fabulous fe

Over 30 exquisite ideas for sophisticated home décor and stunning accessories

PROJECT EDITOR: Meriem Varone
EDITORIAL CO-ORDINATOR: Valérie Gendreau
EDITOR: Sylvie Hano
PROOFREADING: Joëlle Guyon-Vernier
LAYOUT DESIGN: Killiwatch
LAYOUT AND ILLUSTRATIONS: Killiwatch
PHOTOGRAPHY: Fabrice Besse
STYLIST: Sophie Bester
COVER: Killiwatch - Véronique Laporte
MOCK-UPS: Anne Raynaud

PHOTOENGRAVING: Arts Graphiques du Centre

A DAVID & CHARLES BOOK
Copyright © Dessain et Tolra / Larousse 2006
Originally published in France as *Feutre La Déco en douceur*
First published in the UK in 2007 by David & Charles

David & Charles is an F+W Publications Inc. company
4700 East Galbraith Road
Cincinnati, OH 45236

A catalogue record for this book is available from the British Library.

ISBN-13: 978-0-7153-2646-6 paperback
ISBN-10: 0-7153-2646-5 paperback

Printed in China by Shenzhen Donnelley Printing Co Ltd
for David & Charles
Brunel House   Newton Abbot   Devon

Visit our website at www.davidandcharles.co.uk

David & Charles books are available from all good bookshops;
alternatively you can contact our Orderline on 0870 9908222 or
write to us at FREEPOST EX2 110, D&C Direct, Newton Abbot, TQ12 4ZZ
(no stamp required UK only); US customers call 800-289-0963 and
Canadian customers call 800-840-5220.

fabulous felt

Over 30 exquisite ideas for sophisticated
home décor and stunning accessories

SOPHIE BESTER

WITH PHOTOGRAPHY BY
FABRICE BESSE

D&C
David and Charles

For my daughter Laura
For my husband Claude
For my friend Judith

Special thanks to all those who helped in the preparation of this book:
Valérie Côme, Mélanie Guegen, Fabrice Besse, Patrick and my mother.

Thanks also to all those who loaned items for the designs and photography:
Entrée des Fournisseurs, Lefranc & Bourgeois, Bohin, Loisirs et Création, Pébéo, Mokuba,
DMC, Moline, Rougié et Plé, Éléonore Déco, Bougies La Française, Chehoma, Comptoir de Famille,
Jardin d'Ulysse, Athezza, Hervé Gambs and... Frédérick and Marie-Christine Achdou.

FOREWORD

I am one of that generation of schoolgirls who were educated in the finer details of how to sew buttonholes and make up round collars. I have only bad memories of my school sewing career. I can hear those dreaded words 'you've messed that up!' even now.

Yes, hems were fiddly and no, I couldn't sew them properly; I loved fabrics yet I couldn't master the practical side. As time went on I began to feel a twinge of regret, until the day my fairy godmother put a piece of felt in my path.

At first glance it looks nothing special – ordinary, almost – and something of a wallflower next to all the fancy fabrics that sparkle right off their rolls. But to the discerning crafter felt is as soft as velvet, as warm as wool and has a delightfully modest richness about it.

It was love at first sight. Felt would turn out to be my Cinderella story. It has surpassed all my expectations. It can be cut, embroidered, painted and assembled with uncanny ease, and never ceases to impress with its outstanding range of uses.

Whoever would have thought that creating could be so simple?
A child, I'm sure.

SOPHIE BESTER

CONTENTS

INTO THE WOODS

BACK TO NATURE

Woven or synthetic felt?

There are two kinds of felt. Woven felt is entirely natural and is made exclusively from wool fibres. Woven felt can be used both on its right side and its wrong side, which tends to be paler and lightly mottled. To make the beaded tieback on page 26 the front and back of one piece of woven felt were used to give different shades of green. Natural materials are always thought of as superior, but woven felt and synthetic felt each have their advantages and disadvantages. Synthetic felt has long been associated with craftmaking in schools. Today it comes in an enormous range of colours, with shades as subtle and as intense as those of woven felt.

Because synthetic felt is relatively thin, it is not especially strong. This does, however, make it an excellent candidate for curved flower heads, for soft and floaty effects, and for giving the impression of movement. It is inexpensive and recommended for use in one-off projects, such as the party bags on page 82, or purely decorative objects, like the frosted wreath on page 42.

Woven felt is heavier, thicker and has a more compact texture. It is ideal for making up designs with lace-effect cut-outs and for intricately cut shapes. It is also suitable for creating pieces with a longer life. A tieback or pouffe made from synthetic felt will not last long. Synthetic felt is not very wear-resistant: the tieback will start to lose its shape before long and you will hardly have had the chance to sit down before the surface of the pouffe starts to pill.

To avoid unwelcome surprises, stick to the materials quoted in this book because they have been chosen to suit the purpose, life expectancy and upkeep of the projects. Synthetic felt cannot tolerate washing whereas woven felt can be dry-cleaned or washed at 30°C (86°F), for example. The long time it takes to make up the iris throw on page 32 will be worth it because it can be washed again and again and will last a very long time. Remember to check that the different parts you use in your designs (buttons, sequins, glue, ribbons and paint, etc.) can also withstand washing or dry-cleaning.

Cutting and sticking

Cutting and sticking are the two essential techniques used in the designs in this book.

CUTTING TOOLS

You should invest in high-quality equipment and buy one pair of scissors for each type of material you wish to cut. There are two types of all-purpose scissors.

General-purpose fabric scissors are used for cutting out large motifs in woven or synthetic felt; general-purpose paper scissors are used for cutting out templates from tracing paper, Bristol board and card.

Embroidery scissors are essential for intricate work and are the only scissors that allow precision cutting of woven and synthetic felt. These scissors are small and have sharp pointed tips, giving you good control over close work.

Dressmaking scissors and tailor's shears are used for cutting all other fabrics. Dressmaking scissors should be used on thin fabrics such as lawn and nets, while tailor's shears are ideal for cutting wool cloth. Pinking shears are useful for adding a decorative edge to felt.

Rotary cutters are very practical for cutting perfectly straight lines without nicks. They are ideal for making fringes and for visible straight-edge work that needs to be especially neat. Use a rotary cutter on a cutting mat, sliding it from the bottom to the top along a metal ruler.

GLUES

Fabric glues come in three types. White glue can be bought in a tube or a pot and is ideal for gluing intricate motifs on to small surface areas. This is the only glue that is used on polystyrene. Apply the glue with a paintbrush. General-purpose gel glue comes in a tube and is an all-purpose adhesive that can be used on fabrics. It is fairly strong.

The strongest glues are acetone-based glues that can also withstand washing.

Paints, pastels and gels

SPECIAL EFFECT PAINTS

Paint manufacturers are more inventive than ever and you will find a huge variety of special effect paints – relief, translucent, iridescent, pearlescent, metallic – in the shops. They are usually sold in tubes. These practical paints can be applied directly on to your fabric using an integrated applicator, without the need for a paintbrush. Your greatest enemy as far as these paints are concerned is air! As you squeeze the tube, air bubbles loaded with paint can form and explode all over your work. Try out your paints on scrap felt before using them on your work. This will help you work out how much pressure you need to apply for even and precise work on the design.

FABRIC PAINTS

Fabric paints usually come in small jars. The colours are easy to blend and are applied with a paintbrush. Woven felt absorbs less than synthetic felt but you should always avoid getting your fabric too wet.

For best results paint on two layers, waiting at least three hours between each layer.

To make stencil designs, start by testing the absorbency of your fabric. Hold your brush perpendicular to the stencil and dab the fabric gently. Wash your stencil at regular intervals to prevent staining if you intend to reuse it.

When your paint is dry, iron your felt to set the colours.

GLITTER PAINTS AND GELS

Glitter paint is a coloured paint that contains specks of brightly coloured glitter. In this book it was used to decorate the Moroccan slippers on page 114.

Glitter gel, used on the silver snowflakes on page 54, has a clear base that contains brightly coloured glitter. Both gel and paint are applied using a paintbrush. You may need to paint on several layers. Once dry, coat with a water-based gouache varnish to fix the glitter.

HARD PASTEL STICKS AND PENCILS

Hard pastel sticks and pastel pencils are ideal for adding colour to white felt and they come in a superb range of colours. They have a powdery texture and a very rich pigment. Pencils give a soft outline while sticks are better suited to heavier block shading, even in the palest colours. The toy box on page 68 was coloured using pastel sticks.

Pastels are fragile and should be handled with care. They will snap under too much pressure. Go over the same area several times, building up the layers as you go. Work your colours in one after another, blowing on your work at regular intervals to remove any pastel dust, which may stain. When you have finished, spray on a clear matte fixative designed for pastels. Bear in mind when using pastels that the fixative will make the colours darker.

11

Tracing and transferring templates

Tracing paper allows you to transfer a motif or outline directly on to your fabric without having to cut out a template. You can use tracing paper on light colours, or on dark colours after ironing a piece of white iron-on fabric on to the reverse of the felt. Make sure you transfer your design the correct way round. For example, in the angel stocking on page 40 the stocking points to the left, so you should turn your tracing paper over so it points to the right before copying the second stocking so they fit together like a mirror image. To secure the tracing paper while you are transferring the motif, attach it to the fabric with pins, paperclips or sticky tape.

Some of the designs require templates to draw round. If you only need one copy of a motif, a thick sheet of tracing paper will be perfectly adequate. Trace the motif, cut it out and use it as a template. If you have to draw round a motif outline several times, do not use tracing paper as the edges will quickly become damaged by your fabric pen and your outline will be less precise. Instead, for designs which are intricate and duplicated several times, make a template in Bristol board or card. Lay your template on the reverse of your felt. Draw around the outline with a water-soluble fabric pen with a fine tip. Cut out the felt shape and remove any markings with a damp white cloth.

For dark colours, you could use a white gel pen rather than a fabric pen to mark outlines on fabric that has not been backed with iron-on fabric.

Embroidery stitches

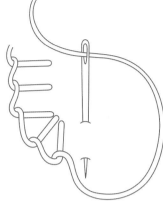

RUNNING STITCH

Running stitch is the easiest stitch to use when attaching two pieces of fabric together or for outlining a motif. The smaller and closer together the stitches, the more secure they will be. At the other end of the scale are longer, tacking-style stitches but these give less secure results. Your stitches should be evenly spaced and the same length as the spaces between them.

BLANKET STITCH

Blanket stitch is used principally to stop the edges of your felt from fraying. It can also be used to sew two pieces of fabric together and gives a more decorative finish than running stitch or backstitch. Space your stitches out according to the effect you want. Sew an oblique stitch to go round corners.

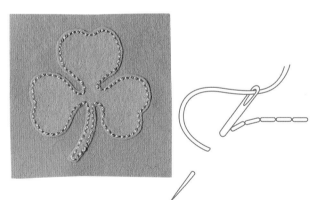

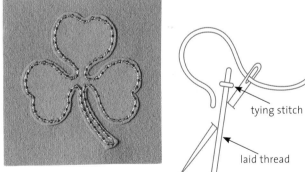

tying stitch

laid thread

BACKSTITCH

This stitch is very secure and can be used to replace a machine stitch because it forms a continuous line along your fabric. It requires a little more practice than running stitch, especially on thick fabrics like felt.

To keep your stitches even, avoid making them too long.

COUCHING

This is one of a wide range of couching stitches. For this technique, a thread is laid along the line of the design on the fabric and it is then secured with small loops known as tying stitches. Couching allows you to use a range of different colours, thread thicknesses and materials. You could use pink perle cotton for the laid thread and violet stranded cotton for the tying stitch, for example.

INTO THE WOODS

Festive heart

MATERIALS REQUIRED

- 30 x 16cm (12 x 6¼in) woven felt in brown
- 16 x 7cm (6¼ x 2¾in) synthetic felt in red
- 20cm (8in) two-tone ricrac braid in red and bronze
- 8 seed beads in red
- 4 heart-shaped silver sequins
- 5 metal snowflakes
- 1 edelweiss button
- Brown sewing thread
- Red perle cotton
- Sewing needle and no.22 chenille needle
- Pins
- Kapok stuffing
- Soft (2B) pencil
- Tracing paper
- Bristol board
- White gel pen
- Pinking shears, paper scissors and embroidery scissors

1. PREPARE THE MOTIFS

Enlarge the heart motif by 140%. Use tracing paper to transfer it on to Bristol board and cut it out. Lay the shape on the reverse of the brown felt and draw round it twice using a gel pen. Do the same on the red felt for the mittens. Cut the four felt shapes out.

2. DECORATE THE MITTENS

Cut a decorative edge along the top of one of the mittens with pinking shears and fold to the right side of the fabric. Sew a piece of ricrac braid across the top of the folded-over fabric with invisible stitches. Sew on four red seed beads along the zigzag edge. In the centre of the mitten, sew on two heart-shaped sequins. Repeat for the other mitten.

3. DECORATE THE HEART

On the right side of one of the hearts, sew on the two mittens with small stitches in brown thread. Using red perle cotton, sew on the five metal snowflakes using a tacking stitch across the base of each arm. Sew on the edelweiss button at the top of the heart, 1cm (⅜in) from the centre point.

4. ASSEMBLY

Using pinking shears, cut a 16 x 2cm (6¼ x ¾in) strip of red felt and sew a length of ricrac along the centre with invisible stitching. Fold the strip in half and sew on to the reverse of the decorated heart. Pin the two hearts back to back and sew them together with blanket stitch (see page 13) using a chenille needle threaded with red perle cotton. About 4cm (1½in) before the end, and without unthreading your needle, stuff the heart with kapok before closing with blanket stitch.

Irish table runner

- 28 x 65cm (11 x 25½in) and 10 x 30cm (4 x 12in) mottled woven felt in red
- 40 x 45cm (15⅝ x 17⅝in) woven felt in brown
- Sheet Bristol board in small squares
- Pencil
- White glue
- Fine-tipped paintbrush
- Flat metal ruler
- Rotary cutter
- Cutting mat
- Paper scissors and embroidery scissors

1. MAKE UP THE TEMPLATES

Using the diagram opposite as a guide, trace shapes A–F on to Bristol board and cut them out. You will use these as templates.

2. CUT OUT THE MOTIFS

Using the reverse of the brown felt for its mottled effect, draw round the templates to create four A shapes, twelve E shapes and twelve F shapes. Cut out using a rotary cutter, metal rule and cutting mat. In the same way draw four B shapes, twelve C shapes and twelve D shapes in the red felt. Cut them out as carefully as you can.

3. ASSEMBLY

Using the diagram as a guide, place all the cut-out shapes on the large red rectangle of felt to make up the motif. Lift each piece carefully without disturbing the other pieces, apply a little glue and stick back down. It is entirely likely that your design will not be completely symmetrical once pieced together. This is normal. Your hand is capable of great things but will never be as accurate as a machine! Some shapes might be a few millimetres out. Slight imperfections will take nothing away from the charm of the design. Quite the opposite!

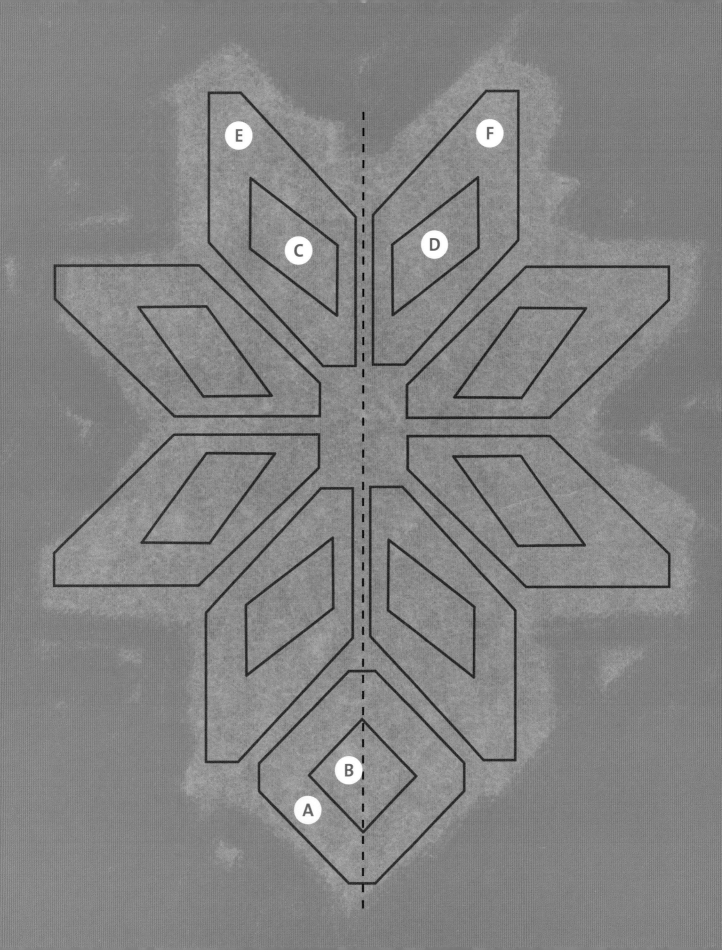

Beaded tieback

MATERIALS REQUIRED

- 2 x 50cm (20in) squares woven felt in fern green
- Seed beads in bronze and iridescent green
- Smaller seed beads in matte gold and iridescent brown
- 1.2m (47in) bronze shoelace cord
- Green sewing thread
- Beading needle
- Pins
- Acetone-based glue
- White glue
- Flat-end brushes: 1 fine-tipped and 1 broad-tipped
- White gel pen
- Paper scissors and embroidery scissors
- Pack of 6 black 14mm (9⁄16in) diameter eyelets and eyelet punch

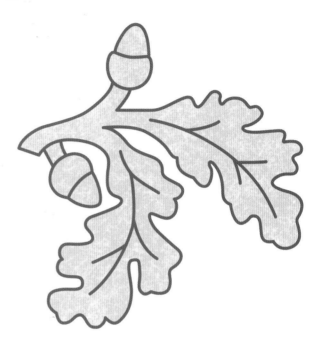

1. PREPARE THE MOTIFS

The tieback uses the wrong side and the right side of the woven felt to give variations in tone. Enlarge the tieback and oak leaf templates by 130%. Place the dotted line of the tieback template on the fold of thick tracing paper and cut out. Pin to the right side of your felt on the diagonal to give you the width you require. Using a gel pen, draw round the outline of the tieback, then cut it out. Do the same on the other square of felt but this time on the reverse. Cut out two oak leaf templates from thick tracing paper and pin them on to the wrong side of the felt. Draw round the outlines and cut out.

half of the tieback
template to be enlarged

2. MAKE UP THE MOTIF

Start by sewing some of the brown beads very close together in the centre of the acorn cup. Mix up your bronze and iridescent green beads and add beads from this bronze and green mix to the base of the acorn cup. Finish by sewing matte gold beads on to the top of the acorn. Decorate all the acorns in this way. Lay the two oak leaf motifs on the right-side felt tieback and mark where they will go with pins. Using a fine-tipped paintbrush, apply white glue to the backs of the motifs, but not to the acorns. Place them on the markings. Apply pressure with the palm of your hand for five minutes. Lift up your acorns one at a time and apply a little acetone-based glue to the back of each one. Leave to dry for one hour.

3. PUT THE TIEBACK TOGETHER

Using a broad-tipped paintbrush, apply a generous amount of white glue to the wrong-side felt tieback, leaving the scalloped edge without glue. Place the decorated right-side tieback on top, leaving 1cm (³⁄₈in) of the wrong-side tieback showing at the bottom. Leave to dry for two hours.

Attach three eyelets to each end of the tieback, 2cm (³⁄₄in) from the edge. Follow the instructions provided with your eyelet kit. Thread a shoelace into the eyelets to tie the tieback on the curtain.

Pansy photo mount

MATERIALS REQUIRED

- 30cm (12in) square foam board
- 30cm (12in) square woven felt in dark orange
- 4 x 18cm (7in) squares woven or synthetic felt in maroon, pale pink, purple and raspberry
- 1.4m (55in) frilled organdie ribbon 4cm (1½in) wide in raspberry
- 1.4m (55in) frilled organdie ribbon 6cm (2⅜in) wide in blue pearlized brown
- Flower-shaped button
- 5 flower-head upholstery tacks
- Sewing thread to match your ribbons and felt
- Sewing needle
- Small pot raspberry acrylic paint
- Fine-tipped paintbrush
- 2 stick-on hooks
- 30cm (12in) brass wire
- Multi-purpose gel glue
- Soft (2B) pencil
- Tracing paper
- Bristol board
- Very fine-tipped black felt tip pen
- Paper scissors and embroidery scissors

1. PREPARATION

Using a fine-tipped paintbrush, paint the four edges of the foam board square with raspberry acrylic paint. Leave to dry. Place the narrow raspberry organdie ribbon over the wider ribbon and sew the two together along the edge using a running stitch (see page 13). Enlarge the small and large pansy petals by 115% and copy them on to tracing paper. Using a fine felt tip pen, transfer the motifs on to a sheet of Bristol board.

Cut out the petals to make four small and one large pansy. Trace all the shapes on to the different coloured felts, varying the colours as you go. Each pansy should have five petals in three different colours.

2. CREATE THE BASE

Sew the length of stitched together ribbons around the square of orange felt 2mm (³⁄₃₂in) from the edge using a running stitch. When you reach the last corner, cut the ends of the two ribbons on the diagonal and join them together. Apply glue to the foam board and lay the orange felt square on top. Smooth to prevent creases.

3. ASSEMBLE THE SMALL PANSIES

Piece the five small pansies together by gluing the petals to one another. Use the diagram as a guide. Leave to dry. Apply a little glue under the head of one of the upholstery tacks and push it into the centre of the flower.

4. ASSEMBLE THE LARGE PANSY

To piece together the button pansy, glue the five large petals together as described in step 3. When the flower is dry, place it right side up on a piece of felt in the colour of your choice. Trace the outline of the pansy on to the felt using a thin felt tip pen. Cut it out just inside the line. Sew a flower-shaped button into the centre of the pansy. Attach the remaining organdie ribbon around the underside of the flower, so that it sticks out a little. Take the felt pansy shape you have just cut out and attach it to the underside of your ribbon with a couple of stitches. The flower should have volume and be life-like. To give the petals a gentle wavy effect, add a little glue either side and under the button and pinch the felt together at the centre. Glue an upholstery tack to the reverse of the flower.

Pin all the pansies to the foam board and tuck photographs or postcards behind them.

5. FINISHING TOUCHES

Attach the two stick-on hooks to the back of the foam board square 12cm (4¾in) from the top and about 16cm (6¼in) apart. Join the two hooks with a length of brass wire.

Iris throw

MATERIALS REQUIRED

- 140cm (55in) square woollen throw in purple heather
- 2 x 50cm (20in) squares woven felt in pale pink
- 2 x 50cm (20in) squares woven felt in mahogany
- Thread to match your felt
- Tacking thread
- Sewing needle
- Pins
- Spray mount adhesive
- 60cm (24in) ruler
- Soft (2B) pencil
- Tracing paper
- 4 sheets Bristol board 21 x 30cm (8¼ x 12in)
- Water-soluble fabric pen
- Paper scissors
- Dressmaking scissors and embroidery scissors

1. PREPARE THE THROW

Use dressmaking scissors to cut your throw fabric carefully into a 130cm (51in) square. Draw a line 4cm (1½in) from the edge all the way around the square with the fabric pen. Tack along this line.

2. MAKE THE IRISES

Enlarge the four iris motifs by 240%.

Copy them on to tracing paper and transfer them on to the sheets of Bristol board. Carefully cut out all the shapes using paper scissors. Lay out the felt squares, right side down, and position the templates on the felt in such a way that you are able to cut out five irises from a 50cm (20in) square. The irises are numbered in the diagram on page 34.

Cut out the following from the pale pink felt:

    2 x iris 1
    4 x iris 2
    2 x iris 3
    2 x iris 4

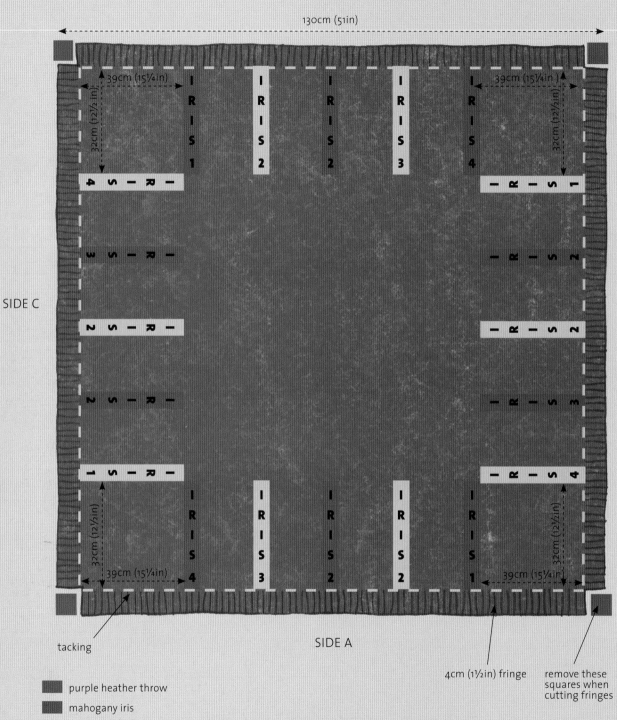

SIDE B

130cm (51in)

39cm (15¼in)

32cm (12½in)

IRIS 1

IRIS 2

IRIS 2

IRIS 3

IRIS 4

39cm (15¼in)

32cm (12½in)

IRIS 4

IRIS 3

IRIS 2

IRIS 2

IRIS 1

4 S I R I

3 S I R I

2 S I R I

2 S I R I

1 S I R I

I R I S 1

I R I S 2

I R I S 2

I R I S 3

I R I S 4

SIDE C

SIDE D

SIDE A

32cm (12½in)

39cm (15¼in)

32cm (12½in)

39cm (15¼in)

tacking

4cm (1½in) fringe

remove these
squares when
cutting fringes

purple heather throw

mahogany iris

pale pink iris

tacking

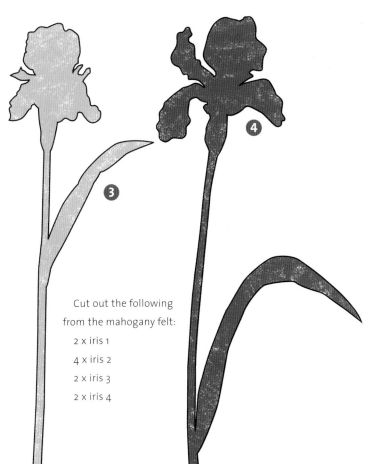

Cut out the following
from the mahogany felt:

2 x iris 1

4 x iris 2

2 x iris 3

2 x iris 4

4. SEW ON THE IRISES

Decide which edge of the throw you will sew your flowers
on to first. Remove the pin from the first iris. Spray a little
adhesive on to the reverse and stick it back into position.
The glue will help to hold the flower in place while you
sew a small backstitch around it in thread to match the
colour of the felt (see page 13). You should finish one edge
before starting the next as this will allow you to sort out
any problems that occur.

5. MAKE THE FRINGES

When you have sewn on all the irises, use a pair of
dressmaking scissors to cut 1cm (⅜in) wide fringes 4cm
(1½in) in length. At each of the corners, remove a small
4cm (1½in) square as shown in the diagram. Remove the
tacking stitches. Because this throw is made of wool, it
should be dry-cleaned.

3. POSITION THE IRISES

Lay the throw out flat on a table and position the irises
on top, using the diagram as a guide. The bases of the
stems should lie 4mm (⁵⁄₃₂in) above the tacking line.
The important thing to remember when positioning the
flowers is not so much getting the distance even between
each flower but rather alternating the colours and shapes,
because this will give a dynamic feel to your design. Once
they are in position, pin all the irises on to the throw.

Cuckoo clock

MATERIALS REQUIRED

- 40 x 21cm (15⅝ x 8¼in) synthetic felt in red
- 40 x 28cm (15⅝ x 11in) synthetic felt in maroon
- 40 x 15cm (15⅝ x 6in) woven felt in dark brown
- 10cm (4in) square synthetic felt in taupe
- 10cm (4in) square synthetic felt in light brown
- 40 x 28cm (15⅝ x 11in) heavyweight iron-on fabric
- 40cm (15⅝in) square lightweight iron-on fabric
- 70cm (27½in) two-tone ricrac braid in red and bronze
- 26cm (10³⁄₁₆in) braid in red and white
- 1 large and 2 small heart-shaped buttons
- 3 copper-coloured mother-of-pearl beads
- 22 assorted charms and 2 miniature clogs

- 1 D-ring picture hanger
- Thread to match your felt
- Sewing needle
- Pins
- Kapok stuffing
- White glue
- Fine-tipped paintbrush
- Soft (2B) pencil
- Tracing paper
- Ruler
- Embroidery scissors
- Iron

dark brown

A

dark brown

light brown

taupe

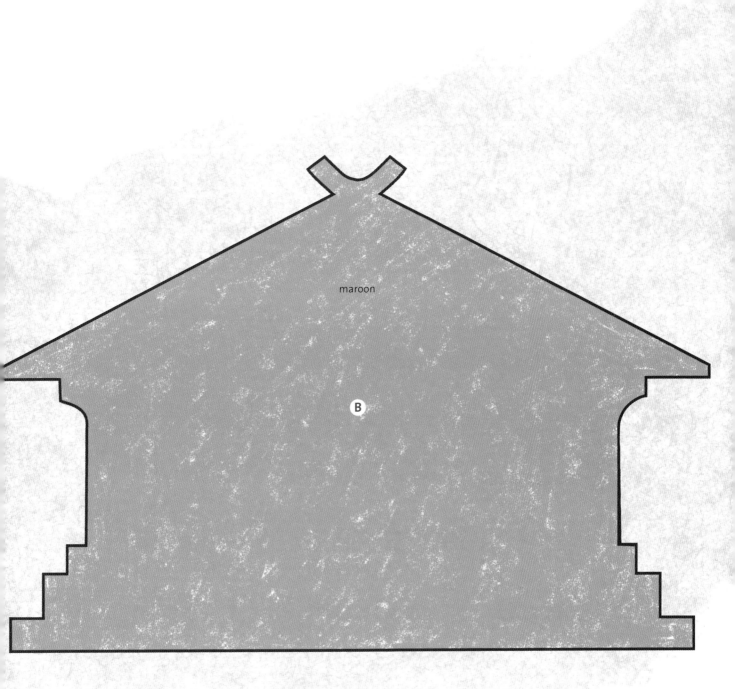

maroon

B

1. CUT OUT THE MOTIFS

Enlarge all the templates that make up the cuckoo clock by 200%, – the roof, middle section and base as well as the Christmas tree, the squirrel and the edelweiss and its leaves. Copy the enlarged motifs on to tracing paper. Use a hot iron to iron heavyweight iron-on fabric on to the maroon felt and the lightweight iron-on fabric on to all the other pieces of synthetic felt and the reverse of the dark brown woven felt. Use the tracing paper to transfer the motifs on to the iron-on fabric. Use the colours on the diagrams as a guide. Make two copies of the squirrel remembering to turn your tracing paper over to give you two mirror image squirrels. Cut the motifs out.

C
red

D
red

red

2. ASSEMBLY

Using the diagram below as a guide, start by attaching the dark brown roof (A) to the maroon middle section (B) using a running stitch along the straight edge (see page 13). Use the same stitch to attach the red felt base of the cuckoo clock (D) to the bottom of the maroon felt (B).

Attach ricrac braid over the join between the red and maroon felts with invisible stitches.

ricrac braid

A

C

B

D

ricrac braid

3. ADD THE MOTIFS

Apply a little glue to the two squirrels, stick them in the centre of the Christmas tree (C) and use a small running stitch to secure each squirrel. Attach ricrac braid along the edge of the felt below the squirrels using invisible stitching, folding the ends of the braid to the back of the red felt. Sew on three heart-shaped buttons. Apply a little glue to the red Christmas tree and position it to fit under the roof as shown in the diagram. Sew a couple of invisible stitches at the end of each branch to secure. Sew the edelweiss to the centre of piece D using the three copper-coloured mother-of-pearl beads. To attach the three leaves, sew a running stitch for approximately 1.5cm (⅝in) along the centre of each leaf.

4. DECORATE THE CLOCK

Spread out the charms evenly over the middle section of the cuckoo clock. When you are pleased with the arrangement sew them on. Sew on the two miniature clogs under the edelweiss. Enlarge the heart template by 200%, trace and copy it four times in maroon felt. Cut them out. Trace and cut out two smaller hearts the size of the template in red felt. Sew a small red heart on to a maroon heart using small stitches. Cut a 10cm (4in) length and a 16cm (6¼in) length of red and white braid. Sew one end of each length of braid on to the reverse of a decorated heart. Pin each decorated heart on to a blank heart and sew them together using blanket stitch (see page 13). Just before finishing, push a little kapok stuffing inside the heart and then complete the blanket stitching. Attach the other ends of the braids to the reverse of the cuckoo clock at the bottom, each side of the point. To position the D-ring, which you will use to hang up your cuckoo clock, on your fabric make a mark on the reverse, 4cm (1½in) down from the top of the cuckoo clock. Measure the width at this point to determine the exact centre. Attach the ring with a couple of stitches.

BACK TO NATURE

Heart candleholder

MATERIALS REQUIRED

- 8cm (3¼in) diameter glass jar, 9cm (3½in) tall
- 9 x 25.5cm (3½in x 10in) woven felt in beige
- 12cm (4¾in) square woven felt in ivory
- 11cm (4⅜in) square lightweight iron-on fabric
- White glue
- Fine-tipped paintbrush
- Ivory sewing thread
- Sewing needle
- Soft (2B) pencil
- Tracing paper
- Embroidery scissors
- Iron

1. MAKE UP THE MOTIF

Start by measuring the height and circumference of your jar. The model here was made using a jar 9cm (3½in) high and 25.5cm (10in) in circumference. (For a larger jar you will need to increase the dimensions of the beige felt.) Iron the lightweight iron-on fabric on to the reverse of the square of ivory felt. Trace the heart motif and then transfer the motif on to the iron-on fabric.

2. CUT OUT THE MOTIF

Carefully cut round the outside of the heart with a pair of embroidery scissors. Cut out the shaded sections inside the heart with care, using the diagram as a guide.

3. ASSEMBLE THE MOTIF

Trace the heart motif outline on to the reverse of the rectangle of beige felt making sure it is centred. Draw a line 3mm (⅛in) inside the outline and cut along this line using embroidery scissors. Lay the felt right side up and use a paintbrush to apply glue round the heart's edge.

Place the cut-out ivory heart gently on top. Apply a little pressure for a few minutes, then leave to dry for at least half an hour.

4. ASSEMBLE THE CANDLEHOLDER

Sew a small blanket stitch (see page 13) all the way around the heart in ivory thread. This will keep the heart secure, even if the heat from the candle melts the glue. Turn your strip of felt on to the reverse, overlapping the edges a little. Secure with a row of small stitches. Turn the finished candleholder cover right side out.

5. FINISHING TOUCHES

Slide the cover over the jar. The felt cover may slide around if it is too large for your jar. If this is the case, carefully lift parts of the cut-out felt heart a little at a time and apply a little glue with a paintbrush. Hold against the jar for three minutes. Leave to dry for two hours before putting a tealight into the jar.

Angel Christmas stocking

MATERIALS REQUIRED

- 50 x 40cm (20 x 15⅝in) woven felt in ivory
- 50 x 40cm (20 x 15⅝in) iron-on fabric
- 50 x 5cm (20 x 2in) sticky-backed synthetic felt in white
- 11cm (4½in) square synthetic felt in white
- 20cm (8in) silver braid
- Seed beads in silver
- 3 metal snowflakes
- Tassel
- Medium-fine silver thread
- 2mm (³⁄₃₂in) thick silver thread
- Sewing thread in white and ivory
- Sewing needle and beading needle
- Pins
- Snowflake punch
- Fabric glue
- Tracing paper
- Soft (2B) pencil
- Water-soluble fabric pen
- Paper scissors and embroidery scissors
- Iron

1. MAKE UP THE STOCKINGS

Enlarge the stocking template by 185% and cut it out. Trace the shape twice on to the reverse of the ivory felt using a fabric pen, turning the template over for the second shape so that the two stockings are mirror images of each other. Cut them out using embroidery scissors. Repeat this process with the iron-on fabric, making the outline 1.5cm (⅝in) smaller. Iron the iron-on fabric stockings on to the reverse of the felt stockings using a hot iron. Cut two rectangles 16 x 9cm (6¼ x 3½in) in ivory felt for the flaps.

2. CREATE THE MOTIFS

Attach iron-on fabric to the square of white felt. Enlarge the angel and snowflake motifs by 185%. Trace the angel motif on to the white felt. Trace the outline of the large snowflake on to the reverse of a piece of ivory felt. Cut these motifs out carefully. Punch eight small snowflakes out of the white sticky-backed felt.

3. ATTACH THE PIECES

Using a medium-fine silver thread, sew the silver braid on to the flap at the top of your stocking, folding the excess behind on the back. Glue the large felt snowflake in the centre of the flap and then sew on silver seed beads at regular intervals all over the flap. Glue the angel to the centre of the stocking. For a neater, more permanent finish, sew a small running stitch close to the edge all round the angel (see page 13).

Attach the three metal snowflakes as shown in the diagram using a tacking stitch across the base of each arm. To make the snowflake trails, sew a running stitch in the 2mm (³⁄₃₂in) silver thread.

Remove the backing from the small white snowflakes and glue one to the centre of the large felt snowflake on the flap. Glue the others directly on to the stocking.

4. ASSEMBLY

Pin the decorated stocking and the decorated flap together. Sew across the top, 3mm (⅛in) from the edge. Do the same with the plain stocking and flap. Place the two stockings together and join with glue or a running stitch 3mm (⅛in) from the edge. Sew the tassel inside the stocking in the top right-hand corner.

Frosted wreath

MATERIALS REQUIRED

- 22cm (8⅝in) diameter lampshade ring
- 60 x 50cm (24 x 20in) very thin synthetic felt in white
- Large bag of white feathers
- Faceted beads in transparent plastic
- Seed beads in silver
- 2.1m (2¼yd) organdie ribbon in white
- 2.8m (3yd) organdie ribbon in silver
- Spool of silver brass wire
- White sewing thread
- Sewing needle and beading needle
- Wire cutters to cut the brass wire
- Embroidery scissors

1. MAKE UP THE FLOWERS

To make a wreath 22cm (8⅝in) in diameter you will need about 23 flowers. To make each flower, cut a strip of felt 2.5 x 50cm (1in x 20in). Thread a needle with white thread and knot the end. Sew along the bottom of your strip of felt, using large stitches, then pull gently on the thread to gather the felt. Curl the strip up to make a flower, then finish off but do not cut the thread. Cut a 10cm (4in) length of silver brass wire, thread a clear bead on to it, then bend the wire over the bead and wind it around itself. Push this pistil into the centre of your felt flower head. Trim two feathers to approximately 3cm (1⅜in) and insert into the centre. Holding the flower, pistil and feathers together, sew several stitches with the white thread through all the layers of felt. Make up 23 flowers in this way.

2. MAKE UP THE BOWS

Cut a 10cm (4in) length of silver brass wire and a 30cm (12in) length of organdie ribbon. Make two ribbon loops, pinch the centre between your fingers and wind the brass wire around it to secure your bow. Make up seven white bows and seven silver bows in this way. Cut a 15cm (6in) length of brass wire, thread on a clear bead, bend the wire over the bead and then wind it around itself. Do the same with two other beads, and then twist the three wire stems together. Make up seven three-bead clusters in this way. Bind up seven bunches of two or three feathers on 15cm (6in) lengths of brass wire.

3. PUT THE WREATH TOGETHER

Assemble your wreath on the metal lampshade ring, alternating flowers, ribbons, bead clusters and feathers and winding all the wire stems around the ring. Sew a few small silver beads inside and outside the felt flowers. When you have finished the wreath, attach a bow at the top to hang it up.

Edelweiss flower ball

MATERIALS REQUIRED

- White polystyrene ball 12cm (4¾in) in diameter
- 39 x 30cm (15⅝x 12in) woven felt in ivory
- 37 x 25cm (14½ x 10in) woven felt in beige
- 102 white mother-of-pearl beads
- 1.2m (47in) silver chenille ribbon
- 50cm (20in) organdie ribbon 7mm (⁹⁄₃₂in) wide in white and silver
- 50cm (20in) silver cord
- Pins
- 6 pins with large white heads
- White fabric glue
- White sewing thread
- Beading needle
- Soft (2B) pencil
- Tracing paper
- Bristol board
- Paper scissors and embroidery scissors

1. PREPARE THE FLOWERS

Copy the two motifs on to tracing paper, transfer them on to a piece of Bristol board and cut them out. Using a pencil, draw round the large template on the reverse of the ivory felt and the small template on the reverse of the beige felt, making 34 copies of each shape. Cut out all the shapes just inside the pencil lines. Make a 1.5cm (⅝in) cut down the centre of each beige petal.

2. PUT TOGETHER THE EDELWEISS

Place a beige flower across an ivory flower. Secure the two flowers together with three stitches in the centre. Sew three mother-of-pearl beads in the centre. Cut a 3.5cm (1³⁄₈in) length of silver chenille ribbon and loop it around the three beads. Trim to fit, then secure the ends with four or five small stitches. Repeat for all the other flower heads.

3. PREPARE THE BALL

Make a loop at the centre of the white organdie ribbon and secure it at the top with two large headed pins. Wrap the remaining organdie ribbon on either side around the ball, holding it with a few normal pins. Overlap the ends a little at the base and trim the excess. Remove the pins, glue on the ribbon and leave to dry. Repeat with the silver cord and silver organdie ribbon.

4. ATTACH THE FLOWERS

Place the edelweiss flowers one by one on to the ball, securing them with a pin pushed in halfway in the centre of the flowers. When the flowers are evenly spread over the ball, push the pins in fully.

Winter warmer

MATERIALS REQUIRED

- 25 x 34cm (10 x 13½in) woven felt in beige
- 13 x 33cm (5 x 13in) woven felt in ivory
- 27 x 36cm (11½ x 14⅛in) woven mohair in ecru
- 2m (2¼yd) braid ribbon
- 68cm (26⅝in) synthetic fur 2.5cm (1in) wide in ivory
- White glue
- Fine-tipped paintbrush
- Pins
- Ivory sewing thread
- Sewing needle
- Tracing paper
- Soft (2B) pencil
- Paper scissors and embroidery scissors
- Iron

1. CUT OUT THE MOTIF

Start by tracing the motif using a soft pencil and transfer it on to the reverse of the ivory felt. As the motif is symmetrical, you need only trace one half of the motif which you should then copy twice on the ivory felt. Using the diagram as a guide, cut out the shaded pieces of the motif carefully using a pair of embroidery scissors. Iron the piece of felt with a cool iron.

2. GLUE ON THE MOTIF

Using a paintbrush, apply a little glue to the felt motif and stick it on to the rectangle of beige felt placing it 5mm (³⁄₁₆in) from the top and bottom and 6cm (2³⁄₈in) from the sides. Use the diagram as a guide. Paint on the glue about 2mm (³⁄₃₂in) from the edges of the cutouts. If the glue is too close to the edges you will have problems later because the glue will make the felt too stiff to sew. Leave to dry for at least one hour.

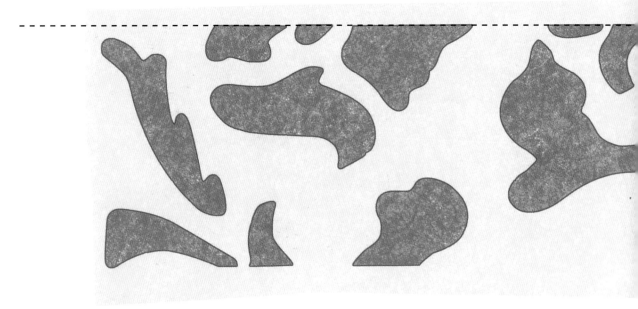

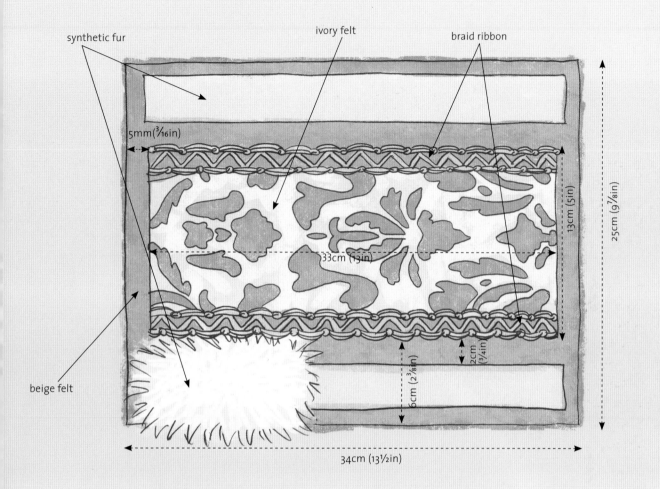

synthetic fur

ivory felt

braid ribbon

5mm(³/₁₆in)

13cm (5in)

25cm (9⁷/₈in)

33cm (13in)

2cm (³/₄in)

6cm (2³/₈in)

beige felt

34cm (13½in)

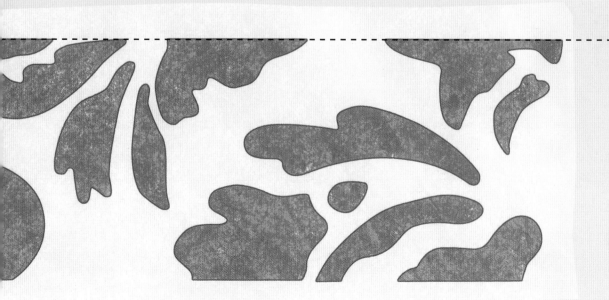

Half-motif to be copied out twice on the ivory felt.

3. EMBROIDERY

Using ivory thread sew a small running stitch close to the edge of all the outlines on the motif (see page 13). Try to keep your stitches even and neat.

4. ATTACH THE BRAID RIBBON

Cut 2 x 34cm (13½in) lengths of braid ribbon. Using a paintbrush, apply glue along the join between the ivory and beige felt pieces and attach the ribbon. It should overlap the ivory felt by about 5mm (³⁄₁₆in). Leave 5mm (³⁄₁₆in) at the ends of the motif.

5. ATTACH THE LINING

Sew a 1cm (³⁄₈in) hem around the edges of the piece of mohair with a running stitch and pin, wrong sides together, to the reverse of the beige felt. Stitch the long felt and mohair edges together. Sew down the edges of the braid ribbon. This will help secure the mohair to the felt, which would have a tendency to move around otherwise. Pin strips of synthetic fur 2cm (³⁄₄in) from the braid and 5mm (³⁄₁₆in) from the ends. Sew on with small stitches.

6. PUT THE HAND WARMER TOGETHER

Assemble your hand warmer with long sides together lengthways so the edges overlap. Pin the two edges together and secure with a running stitch. Turn right side out.

7. FINISHING TOUCHES

Take the remaining length of braid ribbon. Sew small stitches at each end to prevent fraying. Slide the ribbon through the hand warmer and join the two ends by overlapping them by 2cm (³⁄₄in) and sewing them together. Hide the join inside the hand warmer and hang the it around your neck.

Season's Greetings

MATERIALS REQUIRED

- Soft (2B) pencil
- Tracing paper
- Bristol board
- Water-soluble fabric pen
- Paper scissors and embroidery scissors

SWEET HEART

- 16cm (6¼in) square woven felt in ivory
- 16cm (6¼in) square white embroidered netting
- White perle cotton
- Ivory sewing thread
- No.22 chenille needle
- Sewing needle

BIRD CARD

- Greetings card
- 10 x 12cm (4 x 4¾in) woven felt in ivory
- 2 white feathers
- Small tassel
- 25cm (10in) ribbon
- White fabric glue
- Hole punch

1. SWEET HEART

Enlarge the heart shape by 170%. Trace it and transfer the shape on to Bristol board. Cut it out. Place the shape on the reverse of the felt and draw round the outline with a fabric pen. Cut the shape out inside the markings. Do the same with the netting, cutting the shape out carefully with embroidery scissors. Place the net heart on top of the felt heart and trim if necessary. Cut three narrow felt strips 4mm x 12cm (⁵⁄₃₂ x 4¾in) to make three loops and sew them on to the /right side of the felt heart, in the centre at the top. Lay your netting on the right side of the heart

and join the two layers together with blanket stitch using white perle cotton and a chenille needle (see page 13). Leave a small opening and pop a few sweets inside.

2. BIRD CARD

Enlarge the body and wings of the bird by 170%. Transfer these shapes on to Bristol board using tracing paper and then cut them out. Lay each shape on the reverse of the felt and draw round the outlines using a fabric pen. Cut out the shapes inside your markings. Place a feather on each of the wings and, if necessary, trim them so they overhang the wings by about 1cm (³⁄₈in). Carefully apply a little glue to each wing and stick the feathers down. Glue the upper wing under the body. Then glue the lower wing on top of the body. Apply a layer of glue to the back of the bird and attach it to the greetings card. Thread the ribbon through the loop in the tassel. Make a small hole with a punch at the centre of the outside edge of the card. Thread the ribbon through and tie a bow.

Christmas photo album

MATERIALS REQUIRED

- 18.5cm (7¼in) square sketchbook
- 22 x 18cm (8⅝ x 7¼in) woven felt in ivory
- 21 x 50cm (8¼ x 20in) woven felt in beige
- Small and medium-sized silver beads
- Stranded cotton thread in silver
- Tapestry wool skein in beige
- Ivory sewing thread
- Sewing needle and beading needle
- White glue
- Fine-tipped paintbrush
- Soft (2B) pencil
- Tracing paper
- Bristol board
- Water-soluble fabric pen
- Paper scissors and embroidery scissors
- Iron

1. MAKE UP THE LEAVES

To make a Christmas album trace the word Noel and the holly leaf motif. Transfer the holly leaf on to Bristol board, cut it out and draw round it on the ivory felt 16 times. Cut the motifs out inside your markings. Embroider the veins on eight of the leaves using a running stitch and the silver stranded cotton (see page 13). Then sew a small silver bead on to each point – 10 beads per leaf. Join each decorated leaf to a plain leaf with invisible stitching.

2. MAKE UP THE BERRIES

Make up six two-tone holly berries by cutting six 6cm x 4mm (2⅜ x⁵⁄₃₂in) strips of ivory felt and six 5cm x 4mm (2 x ⁵⁄₃₂in) strips of beige felt. Place a small strip on top of a large strip and sew a medium-sized silver bead at the end

of the large strip. Apply glue along the small strip and roll them up with the bead in the middle. Make single-colour berries by cutting three 10cm x 4mm (4 x ⁵⁄₃₂in) strips of beige felt. Apply glue along each strip and roll them up.

3. CREATE THE JACKET

Cut a rectangle of 19.5 x 49cm (7⅝ x 19¼in) in beige felt. Iron a 4cm (1½in) fold at one end. Using ivory thread, sew the flap down on the right side at the top and the bottom using a running stitch close to the edge. Try the jacket for size, folding in the flap at the other end and trimming it to measure 4cm (1½in). Take the sketchbook out of the jacket and sew down the flap in the same way as before.

4. ASSEMBLE THE JACKET

Mark out a 16cm (6¼in) square in the centre of the front felt cover with tacking stitches. Place the Noel template in the square and transfer the lettering on to the felt. Embroider using a couching stitch (see page 13) with the tapestry wool as the laid thread and the silver stranded cotton for the tying stitch. Using the picture as a guide, assemble the holly wreath around the Noel text, making sure you keep within the tacked lines. When you are happy with the design, take out the tacking without disturbing the leaves. Lift each piece carefully and glue with a fine-tipped brush.

4. MAKE AND ATTACH THE BUTTONS

Using the diagram as a guide, insert five pins to mark where the buttons will go. Cover the buttons in mauve felt, following the instructions on the kit. Thread 30cm (12in) perle cotton on to a quilting needle. Next to one of the pins, thread the needle through from the top of the cushion, right through the foam, leaving 10cm (4in) of thread at the surface. Insert the needle 2mm (³⁄₃₂in) from the exit hole, go back through the foam and come out on top of the cushion again. Take off the needle, thread on a button and tie a tight knot. Trim the excess thread. Repeat for the four remaining buttons.

Butterfly lampshade

MATERIALS REQUIRED

(to make about 20 butterflies)

- 36 x 22cm (14³⁄₁₆ x 8⅝in) woven felt in white
- 25cm (10in) squares of embroidered lace in pink, white, lilac, violet and green
- Seed beads in coral pink, white, pistachio, mauve, pink and green
- Sewing thread to match your beads
- Beading needle
- Permanent spray adhesive
- White glue
- Fine-tipped paintbrush
- Soft (2B) pencil
- Thick tracing paper
- Fine-tipped water-soluble fabric pen
- Paper scissors and embroidery scissors

1. MAKE UP BUTTERFLY 1

Trace the butterfly and cut it out. Lay the butterfly template on the reverse of the felt and draw round the outline. Cut it out using embroidery scissors. Remove any markings with a damp cloth.

On another piece of tracing paper, trace the outline of the hatched area of the butterfly and cut it out. Lay this template on the reverse of your felt butterfly and draw round the outline. Using embroidery scissors, cut out the centre and keep. Spray glue on to the reverse of the butterfly and on the right side of the part you have cut out. Place the butterfly with the cut-out on a piece of lace in one colour and place a piece of lace in another colour over the butterfly shape that was cut out. Leave to dry for 30 minutes. Trim any excess lace round the felt shapes.

Hold the two wings of the butterfly created from the cut-out shape in your fingers and sew three small stitches on the reverse in the centre so that the wings are lifted up slightly. Place this part on top of the other butterfly and secure together by sewing on beads to make up the body.

BUTTERFLY 1

BUTTERFLY 3

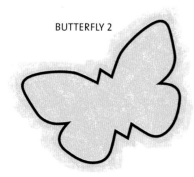

BUTTERFLY 2

2. MAKE UP BUTTERFLY 2 AND BUTTERFLY 3

Trace the butterflies and cut them out. Lay the butterfly templates on the reverse of your felt and draw around the outlines. Cut them out using embroidery scissors. Remove any markings with a damp cloth.

Spray a little glue on to the right side of the butterflies and place pieces of lace in the colour of your choice on top. Leave to dry for 30 minutes. Turn the butterflies over and trim off the excess lace. Sew on seed beads in the colours of your choice to make the bodies.

Butterfly 3 is only needed for lampshades with a diameter equal to or greater than 22cm (8⅝in). It is not used on the 20cm (8in) diameter lampshade shown here.

3. MAKE UP BUTTERFLY 4

Trace the two butterfly templates and cut them out. Place the butterfly templates on the reverse of the felt and draw around their outlines. Cut them out using embroidery scissors. Remove any markings with a damp cloth.

Spray glue on to the right side of each butterfly and glue lace in one colour on to the large wings and lace in another colour on to the small wings. Leave to dry for 30 minutes. Turn the butterflies over and trim the excess lace.

Hold the small wings in your fingers and sew three small stitches on the reverse along the back in the centre to lift them slightly. Secure the small wings to the large wings by sewing on a few beads to form the body.

BUTTERFLY 4

large wings

small wings

4. ASSEMBLE THE LAMPSHADE

Apply glue to the reverse of your butterflies and stick them on to the lampshade. Alternate the different butterflies around the shade. Position them in such a way so that they appear to be flying.

Baby's first book

MATERIALS REQUIRED

- 27cm (10½in) square sketchbook
- 77 x 35cm (30³⁄₁₆ x 13¾in) synthetic felt in sky blue
- 10 x 8cm (4in x 3⅛in) synthetic felt in white
- 7 x 3cm (2¾ x 1⅛in) synthetic felt in pink, pale green, pale yellow and sky blue
- 45cm (17⅝in) velvet ribbon 3mm (⅛in) wide in pink, pale green, pale yellow and sky blue
- Sewing threads to match your felts
- Sewing needle
- Pins
- Cotton wool
- Floral heart stencil or similar
- Fabric paint in titanium white
- Small stencil brush
- Tube of fabric glue
- Sticky tape
- Soft (2B) pencil
- Thick tracing paper
- Fine-tipped fabric pen
- Cutting mat
- Rotary cutter
- Flat metal ruler
- Paper scissors and embroidery scissors
- Iron

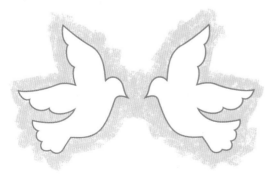

1. MAKE UP THE COVER

Using a rotary cutter and cutting mat, cut a rectangle measuring 75 x 33cm (29½ x 33in) in sky blue felt. Using the diagram as a guide, fold over 9cm (3½in) of felt on the left side of the rectangle, right sides together. Sew the flap down across the top and bottom 3cm (1⅛in) from the edge. Insert the book cover into the flap, fold it round the book and fold in the remaining fabric. Trim the second flap to measure 9cm (3½in). Remove book and sew down the flap as before. Cut off the four corners of your fabric to prevent bulkiness and turn the cover right side out.

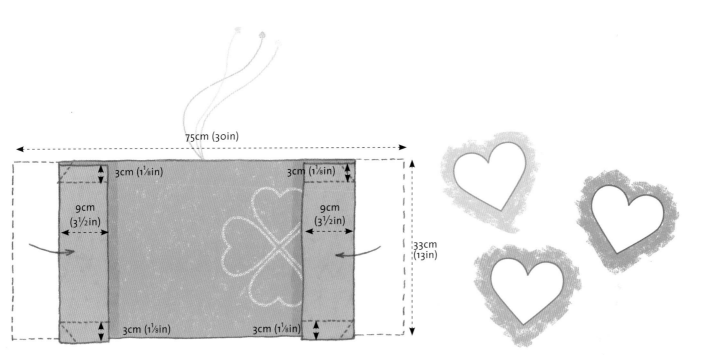

75cm (30in)

3cm (1⅛in)   3cm (1⅛in)

9cm
(3½in)   9cm
(3½in)

33cm
(13in)

3cm (1⅛in)   3cm (1⅛in)

Iron the cover, then sew a small running stitch all the way around it, close to the edge (see page 13). Check to see that the sketchbook fits snugly inside the jacket.

2. PAINT THE MOTIF

Place tracing paper on to your stencil and make four copies of the heart outline only. Cut out all four tracing paper hearts. Lay them in the centre of the front of the cover arranged in the final design and pin them down. Place the stencil on top of one of the tracing paper hearts. Secure on three sides with sticky tape. Lift up the fourth side and remove the tracing paper. Using a stencil brush, apply the paint by dabbing gently (see page 10). Leave the paint to dry thoroughly, then place the stencil on top of the next heart and work in the same way. Repeat the process for all of the hearts and leave to dry.

3. MAKE UP THE BIRDS

Trace the birds and cut out tracing paper templates using paper scissors. Draw round each template twice on the reverse of the white felt. Cut the birds out using embroidery scissors. Glue them on to the cover, using the picture as a guide for positioning them.

4. MAKE UP THE BOOKMARKS

Trace the small heart and cut out the template using paper scissors. Draw round the heart twice on the pink, yellow, green and sky blue felt. Cut out the felt hearts using embroidery scissors. At the centre of one of each of the colour hearts sew the end of a velvet ribbon in the same colour. Place the other half of the heart on top and sew together using blanket stitch in matching sewing thread (see page 13). Before completing the stitching insert a little cotton wool between the two hearts and then finish off the blanket stitch. Sew the four ribbons inside the cover at the centre, making the ribbons different lengths.

Angel baby blanket

MATERIALS REQUIRED

- 20 x 27cm (8 x 10½in) woven felt in white
- 29 x 16cm (11⅜ x 6¼in) woven felt in blue
- 60 x 80cm (23½ x 31⅜in) woollen fabric in off-white
- 60 x 80cm (23½ x 31⅜in) woollen fabric in violet
- Ball of fluffy thread in white
- White sewing thread
- Chenille needle and sewing needle
- Pins
- Feather stencils
- Opaque fabric paint in pearl white
- Opaque fabric paint in white
- Small stencil brush
- Soft (2B) pencil
- Tracing paper
- Bristol board
- Very fine-tipped fabric pen
- Dressmaking scissors and embroidery scissors
- Paper scissors
- Craft knife
- Iron

1. MAKE UP THE MOTIFS

Enlarge the cloud template and the cherub template by 165% and trace them separately. Transfer the motifs on to Bristol board and cut them out carefully using paper scissors. Place the cloud template on the reverse of the blue felt, and the cherub template on the reverse of the white felt. Using a fabric pen, draw round the outlines on to the felt, then cut out each motif using embroidery scissors. Use a craft knife to cut out the slits above and below the cherub's arms cleanly. Remove any markings with a damp cloth.

2. SEW ON THE MOTIFS

On the reverse of each piece of woollen fabric mark a
rectangle 58 x 78cm (22¾ x 30½in) with a fabric pen and
cut it out using dressmaking scissors. Lay the cloud with
the cherub on top towards one corner of the violet blanket.
The top of the cherub's head should be 7.5cm (3in) from
the edge. Pin the two motifs on to the blanket and sew
them on with small running stitches. Using a chenille
needle, sew a couching stitch all the way around the cloud
using doubled lengths of fluffy thread for the laid thread
and white sewing thread for the tying thread (see page 13).

3. PAINT THE FEATHERS

Using the stencils as a guide, trace the shapes of the
different feathers on tracing paper and cut out. Pin the
paper feathers on the blanket, arranging them until you
are happy with the effect. Alternate between small and
large feathers and avoid making the blanket look too busy.
Mix one third pearl white paint with two thirds white
paint in a small saucer. Lay the blanket out on a flat and
stable surface. Remove one of the paper feathers and lay
the corresponding stencil down in its place. Apply a little
paint to the brush and gently dab the paint on to the

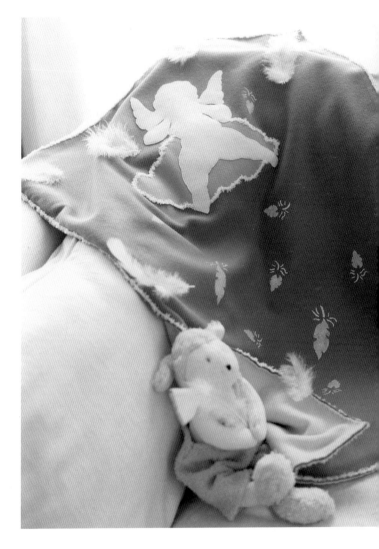

blanket. Work in the same way for all the feathers. Leave
to dry overnight, then iron each feather on the reverse for
several minutes to set the paint.

4. FINISHING TOUCHES

Lay the two blankets one on top of the other, wrong sides
together and pin them at 5cm (2in) intervals along the
edges. Sew the two blankets together all the way around
with a couching stitch using the fluffy thread doubled in
the same way as you did for the cloud.

Toy box

- Round cardboard box 23.5cm (9¼in) in diameter, 16.5cm (6½in) high and 76cm (30in) in circumference
- 3 x 50cm (20in) squares woven felt in white
- 35 x 10cm (13¾ x 4in) woven felt in pale blue
- 35 x 10cm (13¾ x 4in) woven felt in pale green
- 40cm (16in) square heavyweight iron-on fabric
- 8 mini pompoms in white
- A4 sheet of foam board
- Pins
- Hard pastel sticks or pencils in pale green, pale blue, melon and pale yellow
- All-purpose tube paints in crystal effect, pistachio, sky blue and scarlet
- Clear matte fixative for pastels
- 2 tubes fabric glue
- Tube white glue
- Soft (2B) pencil
- Tracing paper
- A4 sheet of Bristol board
- Fabric pen
- Flat metal ruler
- Rotary cutter
- Cutting mat
- Paper scissors and embroidery scissors
- Iron

1. MAKE UP THE TEMPLATES

Enlarge the motifs (leaves, dragonfly, wing, toadstool, snail body) by 155% and then trace them. Transfer them on to Bristol board and cut out all the motifs using paper scissors.

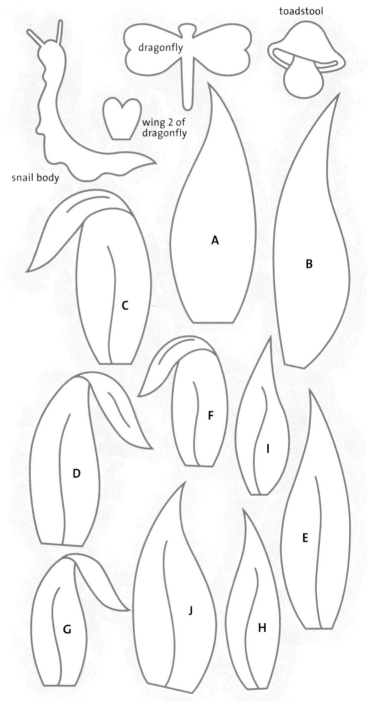

dragonfly

toadstool

wing 2 of dragonfly

snail body

A

B

C

F

I

D

E

J

H

G

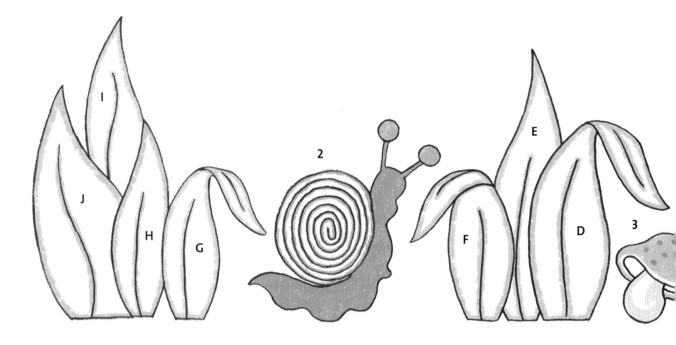

2. MAKE UP THE MOTIFS

Place one square of white felt right side down and lay your template for leaf A on top. Use your fabric pen to draw round its outline twice and label it. This will help you when you come to assemble your design. Repeat, making two copies of each motif, except for the snail, and three copies of the dragonfly and its wings. You will have 20 leaves, two toadstools and three dragonflies. Using embroidery scissors, cut out each motif carefully inside the markings. Remove any fabric pen markings with a damp white cloth, dabbing carefully so as not to remove the letters.

3. ADD COLOUR TO THE MOTIFS

Lay out all the motifs right side up and, using the diagram above and the picture details to help you, colour the edges of the leaves and their veins, the two toadstools and the three dragonflies using hard pastel sticks or pencils (see page 11). Colour half of the mini pompons orange and the rest pink. You will use these for the snail antennae.

Pin all the shapes on to the sheet of foam board. This will make it easy to spray on a layer of pastel fixative. Leave to dry for at least one hour, and repeat. Wait another hour before removing the shapes from the foam board.

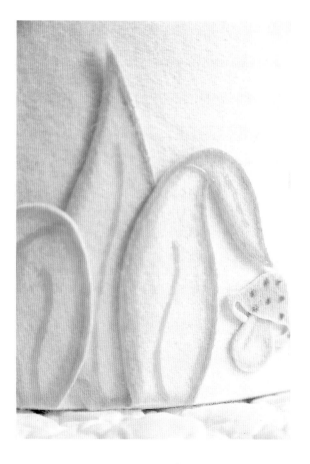

4. MAKE UP THE SNAILS

Prepare strips measuring 4mm x 32cm ($\frac{5}{32}$ x 12¾in) as follows. Cut four in white felt, two in blue felt and two in green felt. Use a metal rule and a rotary cutter on a cutting mat to keep the edges straight. Cut out two rectangles 16 x 14cm (6½ x 5½in) of blue felt and cut each rectangle into two pieces of equal size. Apply glue to the reverse of one of the pieces and glue the other one on top. Do the same with the green felt. Wait 20 minutes until the felt is dry before transferring the snail template twice on to each rectangle using a fabric pen. Cut the four shapes out using embroidery scissors.

Take the four white strips and apply a strip of white glue on top. Glue a green or blue strip on to each of them. Leave to dry for 15 minutes. Turn the strips over and add a little more glue to the other white side and start to roll the two glued strips around themselves, with the white felt inside and the coloured felt on the outside. Work a little at a time, allowing the glue to take hold with every turn you make so that the snail shells are nice and tight.

5. PAINT YOUR MOTIFS

Check that the fixative on the leaves is dry. Lay the leaves out flat and paint around the edges and the central veins in matching tones (sky blue paint on the blue leaves and pistachio on your green leaves). Be careful not to paint too thin a line because when it dries the paint will shrink in size by a third. Dot scarlet paint on to the hoods of the toadstools (see page 10). Leave each motif to dry for at least 12 hours, by which time the paint will have turned clear and you will be able to see the finished colours.

6. ASSEMBLE THE MOTIFS

Using a rotary cutter, cut two strips 38 x 16.5cm (15 x 6½in) in white felt. Lay out one strip right side up and using the diagram as a guide position the different pieces along the bottom. Make sure you keep to the following order, working from right to left: A, B, C, 1, 3, E, D, F, 2, I, J, H, G. When you are happy with the design use white glue to stick them down, noting that some of the pieces overlap. Repeat the process on the second strip. Leave to dry.

7. PUT THE BOX TOGETHER

Take one of the motif strips and coat the reverse in a little
white glue. Put the box on the table and quickly stick your
strip on top, because the paint will react with the glue.
Pull the strip to prevent creasing if necessary. If air bubbles
appear, smooth them out using a clean white cloth. Attach
the second strip in the same way.

8. MAKE THE ROOF

Enlarge the roof template by 180% to make a scalloped
circle 34cm (13⅜in) in diameter. Cut it out carefully. Take a
square of white felt and iron the square of iron-on fabric
on to the reverse with a very hot iron. Place the template
on the felt and secure with a pin at the centre. Draw
around the outline using a fabric pen. Cut the shape out
inside the markings using embroidery scissors. On the
reverse, use a ruler to mark the piece to be cut out. Cut it
out. Apply a little glue along the felt edge of the cut in the
roof and stick the two sides together, matching scallops.
Trim any excess fabric.

Paint dots at regular intervals all the way around the
scalloped edging in scarlet paint. Leave to dry for 12 hours.
Glue the small dragonfly wings on to the large wings by
applying a line of glue close to the straight edge of the
small wings. Glue the three dragonflies on to the roof,
using the pictures as a guide.

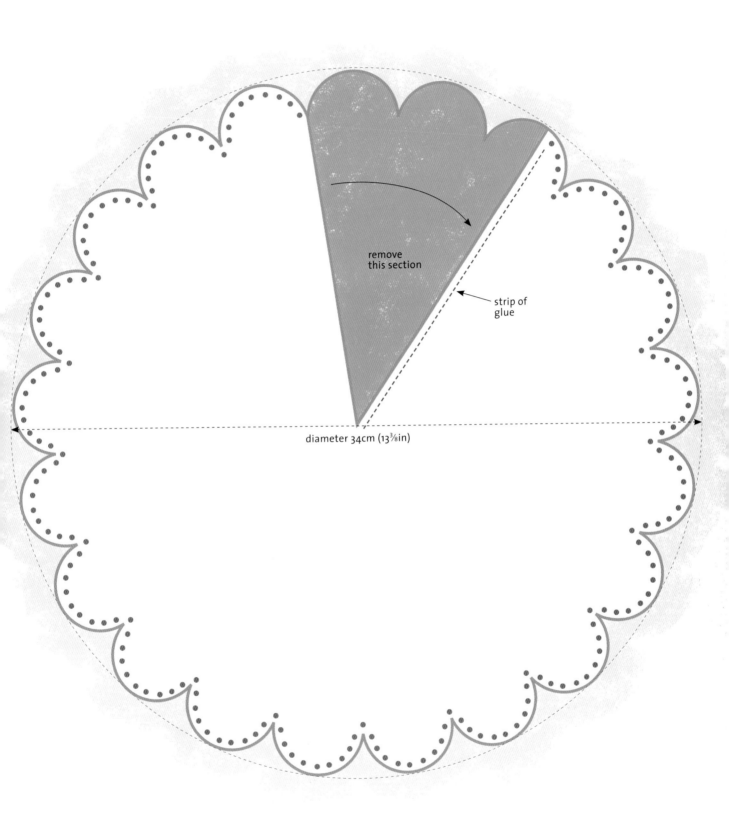

remove
this section

strip of
glue

diameter 34cm (13⅜in)

Doll's vanity case

MATERIALS REQUIRED

- Small pink cardboard case
- 25 x 20cm (9⅞ x 8in) synthetic felt in candy pink
- 16 x 12cm (6¼ x 4¾in) synthetic felt in white
- 10 x 5cm (4 x 2in) synthetic felt in pale blue
- 10 x 5cm (4 x 2in) lightweight iron-on fabric
- Heart-shaped sticker
- 3 medium-sized lilac beads
- 2 flower-shaped sequins in pale pink and 3 in pale blue
- 2 seed beads in white and 9 in pink
- 1 pink sequin
- 14cm (5½in) pleated ribbon 2cm (¾in) wide in pink
- Miniature coathanger
- Sewing thread in pink and white
- Sewing needle
- Pins
- Hole punch
- Fabric glue
- Soft (2B) pencil
- Thick tracing paper
- Very fine-tipped fabric pen
- Paper scissors and embroidery scissors
- Iron

1. MAKE THE TEMPLATES

Trace the clothes motifs (skirt, dress, dress pocket and bikini) and cut them out with paper scissors.

2. MAKE UP THE DRESS

Take the piece of pink felt and cut it into two equal pieces. Place the two pieces one on top of the other and secure with four pins at the top, bottom and sides). Place the dress template on to the felt and draw around the outline using a fabric pen. Cut the dress out using embroidery scissors. Take out the pins and remove any markings. Place the pocket template on to a strip of pink felt. Draw around the outline and cut it out. Sew the pocket on to the centre of one of the dress motifs using a running stitch (see page 13). Place the heart sticker in the centre of the pocket.

Next, sew on three lilac beads down the front of the dress. Place the two dresses back to back one on top of the other and sew them together down the sides using a running stitch. Sew two pale pink flower-shaped sequins on to the shoulders with a white seed bead in the centre of each flower.

3. MAKE THE BIKINI

Iron a piece of iron-on fabric on to one side of the pale blue felt. Place your bikini templates on the iron-on fabric side and draw around the outlines with the fabric pen. Cut out the motifs using embroidery scissors and glue on three pale blue flower-shaped sequins, using the picture as a guide for positions.

4. MAKE UP THE SKIRT

Cut white felt into two equal-sized pieces. Place these pieces one on top of the other and pin them together. Place the skirt template on the felt and draw around the outline with a fabric pen. Cut the skirt out using embroidery scissors. Remove the pins and any markings.

On the front of the skirt, make a belt by attaching a pink

sequin with a pink seed bead in the centre and then sew four small pink beads to the right and four small pink beads to the left of the sequin. Make six little polka dots from a strip of pink felt using a hole punch. Cut the flounced ribbon in half. Glue one piece to the front of the skirt at the bottom. Fold the excess to the back and glue it down. Glue the polka dots on to the front of the skirt. Glue the other length of ribbon to the back piece of the skirt in the same way as the front. Assemble the two parts of the skirt using a running stitch down the sides.

5. ASSEMBLY

Place the clothes and the miniature coathanger on the top of the vanity case. Apply glue to the back of each of the pieces in turn and stick them to the case.

Floral cushion

MATERIALS REQUIRED

- 40 x 50cm (15⅝ x 20in) floral lawn fabric in mauve, pink and green tones
- 40 x 50cm (15⅝ x 20in) lightweight iron-on fabric
- 30 x 23cm (12 x 9in) thin woven felt in pale khaki
- 2 pieces 30 x 23cm (12 x 9in) thin woven felt in almond green
- 40 x 70cm (15⅝ x 27½in) woven felt in lilac
- 100 x 50cm (39¼ x 20in) flat cotton fleece
- Sewing thread in almond green and lilac
- Sewing needle
- Pins
- Punch to make 20mm (¾in), 18mm (¹¹⁄₁₆in), 16mm (⅝in) and 10mm (⅜in) holes
- Hammer
- Cutting mat
- All-purpose gel glue
- Special glue for use on plastics
- Sticky tape
- Blutack
- Sheet of paper
- Soft (2B) pencil
- Tracing paper
- Bristol board
- Fabric pen
- Pair of compasses
- Paper scissors and embroidery scissors
- Iron
- Plastic drum-style stool

1. MAKE UP THE TEMPLATES

Enlarge the template of the large flower by 160%. Join sheets of tracing paper together if necessary with sticky tape and trace the outline of the large flower. Cut the tracing paper template out carefully. Trace the motifs of the two small flowers and copy their outlines on to Bristol board. Cut them out.

2. CUT OUT THE PIECES

Using a very hot iron with the steam setting turned off, iron the iron-on fabric on to the reverse of the floral lawn fabric. Draw round the tracing paper template of the large flower twice on to the reverse of the lilac felt using a fabric pen. Cut out the two flowers. Using compasses, draw a circle 16cm (6½in) in diameter on the Bristol board and cut it out. Place this template on to a piece of almond green felt and draw around it using a fabric pen. Cut it out.

Cut six circles 15cm (6in) in diameter from cotton fleece. Cut out the large flower shape three times from the fleece, making them 1cm (⅜in) smaller.

3. PUT THE LARGE FLOWER TOGETHER

Lay your six 15cm (6in) fleece circles down so that they are overlapping each other. Place one of the lilac felt flowers on top, making sure it is well centred. Then place an almond green felt circle on top. Pin together to keep everything in place while you sew. Sew together using a small running stitch (see p.13) all the way around the centre of the flower using almond green thread. When you have finished, place the flower face down on your work surface and put the three fleece flowers and the second lilac felt flower on top. Pin to secure and, using lilac thread, sew a running stitch right around the petals of the flower.

5. MAKE UP THE SMALL FLOWERS

Use the Bristol board template for the larger of the two flower motifs shown below to draw round on the reverse of the backed floral lawn fabric using a fabric pen. Copy the flower out 24 times. Cut out all the flowers and remove any markings with a damp white cloth.

Using the fabric pen, copy around the Bristol board template for the small flower 12 times on the almond green felt. Cut out the 12 flowers. Repeat this process to cut out 12 small flowers from the pale khaki felt. Remove any markings with a damp white cloth. Using a 20mm (¾in) punch, remove a circle from the centre of the 12 khaki flowers and the 12 almond green flowers. Glue a felt flower on to each floral lawn flower using gel glue.

6. ATTACH THE SMALL FLOWERS

Glue the twenty-four felt and lawn flowers on to the drum stool, alternating the colours and using a special glue designed for plastics. To plan your design use the template to cut out several flower shapes from scraps of coloured paper. Stick them on with Blutack, adjusting their position until you are happy with the overall effect. Remove the paper flowers one by one and glue a felt and floral lawn flower in its place.

4. MAKE UP THE MOTIFS

Using an 18mm (¹¹⁄₁₆in) punch, make twenty discs in khaki green felt. Using a 10mm (⅜in) punch, remove the centre of these discs. Keep twelve of these khaki green felt discs and glue them on to the almond green felt centre of the flower. Using a 16mm (⅝in) punch, make twenty discs in floral lawn fabric. Glue the khaki green 18mm (¹¹⁄₁₆in) felt discs on to the floral discs. Leave to dry for at least 30 minutes. Glue four felt and floral fabric discs on to each flower petal using an all-purpose gel glue.

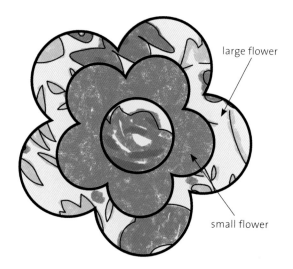

large flower

small flower

78

OVER THE RAINBOW

Party bags

MATERIALS REQUIRED

- 60 x 42cm (23½ x 16½in) tulle netting in orange
- 28 x 21cm (11 x 8¼in) synthetic felt in dusty pink
- 30 x 22cm (12 x 8⅝in) synthetic felt in orange
- 7cm (2¾in) square very thin synthetic felt in pale pink
- 50cm (20in) velvet ribbon 1cm (½in) wide in pale orange
- 65cm (25½in) organdie ribbon 35mm (1⅜in) wide in orange
- 8 white flower-shaped sequins
- 10 seed beads in orange
- Sewing thread and perle cotton in orange
- Sewing needle and beading needle
- Gold glitter gel and paintbrush
- Fabric glue (optional)
- Small heart-shaped punch
- Pencil and tracing paper
- Bristol board
- Water-soluble fabric pen
- Paper scissors and embroidery scissors

1. PREPARE YOUR PIECES

Enlarge the tulip shape by 175% and trace it on to Bristol board. Cut it out. Trace the two dragonflies and transfer them on to Bristol board. Cut them out. Place the tulip template on the orange felt and draw round the outline twice using a fabric pen. Draw round the templates for the large and small dragonflies on the orange felt in the same way. Cut out the four shapes. Paint a layer of glitter gel over the wings of the large dragonfly. Leave to dry for at least four hours.

3. PARTY BAG

Cut the piece of tulle in two. Sew the small dragonfly in the bottom right-hand corner of the dusty pink felt. Sew two orange beads on to the head of the large dragonfly to make the eyes. Sew it on to a piece of tulle using orange perle cotton, leaving the wings free. Sew a few horizontal stitches over the body of the dragonfly. Place the rectangle of tulle with the dragonfly over the rectangle of pink felt with the dragonfly and place the second tulle rectangle underneath. The tulle pieces are slightly larger than the felt. Join the three pieces at the base and sides. At the top, only join together the felt and the piece of tulle with the dragonfly. Put small treats between the felt and the other layer of tulle. Tie the bag with a large bow using the orange organdie ribbon.

2. TULIP POUCH

Using the punch, make nine hearts in pale pink felt. Make three small flowers on one of the tulip shapes by sewing on three hearts together three times. Sew a white sequin into their centres, held in place by an orange bead. Sew one or two white sequins between the felt flowers with an orange bead. Cut the velvet ribbon in two. Sew a length of ribbon on to the wrong side of each of the felt tulips, either side of the centre petal, to form two handles. Join the two tulips together with fabric glue or a small running stitch 2mm (3⁄32in) from the edge (see page 13).

Bear cub Alice bands

MATERIALS REQUIRED

(to make one white bear cub)

- 1 Alice band
- 14 x 6cm (5½ x 2½in) woven felt in white
- 4cm (1¾in) square synthetic felt in violet
- 5cm (2in) square floral lawn fabric
- 24 x 6cm (9½ x 2⅜in) lightweight iron-on fabric
- 2 Swarovski beads in violet
- 1 bugle bead in violet
- White sewing thread
- 20cm (8in) stranded cotton in black
- Sewing needle and beading needle
- Kapok stuffing
- Extra-strong glue
- White glue
- Very fine-tipped paintbrush
- Soft (2B) pencil
- Thick tracing paper
- Fabric pen
- Paper scissors and embroidery scissors
- Iron

1. CUT OUT THE PIECES

Trace the bear templates on to tracing paper (head with collar, collar alone, insides of the ears, two nose pieces and the bow) and cut them out. Using a hot iron with the steam setting turned off, iron the iron-on fabric on to the reverse of the pieces of felt and floral lawn fabric. Lay the templates on the reverse of the fabrics, using the photo as a guide. Draw around the outlines using a fabric pen, then cut out the shapes with embroidery scissors. Cut the head motif out twice. Remove any markings using a damp white cloth.

2. PUT THE HEAD TOGETHER

Take one head motif and, using the picture as a guide, glue the ears and two nose pieces on to the front. Sew two Swarovski beads on for the eyes and embroider the bottom of the nose and the mouth with two strands of black stranded cotton, by sewing three straight stitches. Place the second head motif under the first and, using white sewing thread, sew round the outside with a fairly tight blanket stitch (see page 13). About 2cm (¾in) before finishing slide a little kapok stuffing inside to give the head some body but without making it too bulky. Finish off with blanket stitch.

3. FINISHING TOUCHES

Apply a little glue to the reverse of the floral lawn collar with your paintbrush and glue it to the white felt collar, matching the curved edges. Sew a bugle bead to the centre of the floral bow and then apply glue to the reverse of the bow and stick it down on the diagonal near the bear's ear. Apply extra-strong glue to a 3cm (1⅛in) length of the Alice band and stick the bear on top. Hold in the bear in place until the glue has set.

Strawberry hairclips and hair bands

MATERIALS REQUIRED

(to make 2 small hairclips or 2 hair bands)

- 2 small hairclips (or 2 elasticated bands)
- 11 x 5cm (4¼ x 2in) woven felt in fuchsia
- 3 x 7cm (1⅛ x 2¾in) woven felt in purple
- 18 seed beads in white
- Sewing thread in fuchsia and white
- Beading needle and sewing needle
- Kapok stuffing (or cotton wool)
- Fabric glue
- Pencil
- Thick tracing paper
- Very fine-tipped water-soluble fabric pen
- Paper scissors
- Embroidery scissors

1. MAKE UP THE TEMPLATES

Trace the strawberry and leaf motifs on to tracing paper and cut them out carefully. Cut the fuchsia felt into two pieces of equal size. Place the strawberry template on the reverse of your felt and make two copies using a fabric pen and turning your tracing paper over to give you two mirror images of the strawberry. Place the leaf template on the reverse of the purple felt and draw round the outline. Cut out the three shapes using embroidery scissors.

2. DECORATE THE STRAWBERRY

Take one of the strawberries and, before sewing your beads on, work out where you will place the leaf at the top to avoid sewing on a bead underneath the leaf.

Sew on nine white seed beads using a beading needle and white sewing thread.

3. PUT THE STRAWBERRY TOGETHER

Place the two parts of the strawberry together and sew round the edge with blanket stitch using fuchsia thread (see page 13). Just before you finish off, stuff the strawberry with kapok stuffing. Be generous: your strawberry should look firm and plump and should not flatten out when you come to wear it. Complete the stitching. Glue the purple leaf to the top of the strawberry.

4. ASSEMBLY

Sew the strawberry on to the centre part of the hairclip. To save time you could attach the strawberry using extra-strong glue, but this will make it less robust.

5. LARGE HAIRCLIPS

The number of strawberries you make up will depend on the length of your hairclip. For an 8cm (3⅛in) hairclip you will need three large or four small strawberries. Vary the colours of the strawberries and beads as you go. A strawberry sewn to a decorative elastic band makes a matching hair band.

for the small hairclips
and hair band

for the large hairclip

Puppy gloves

MATERIALS REQUIRED

- 1 pair fuchsia knitted gloves
- 15 x 22cm (6 x 8⅝in) woven felt in bright red
- 15 x 20cm (6 x 8in) lightweight iron-on fabric
- 1 box small bugle beads in fuchsia
- 18 x 5mm (¼in) crystal bicone beads in fuchsia
- 2 black bugle beads
- Sewing thread in fuchsia and bright red
- Long beading needle
- Pencil
- Thick tracing paper
- Fine-tipped fabric pen
- Paper scissors and embroidery scissors
- Iron

1. PREPARE THE MOTIFS

Trace the dog and bone and cut them out. Using a very hot iron with the steam setting turned off, iron the iron-on fabric on to the reverse of the rectangle of felt. Use a fabric pen to draw round the templates and make four copies of the dog on the iron-on fabric side of your felt and six copies of the bone. Remember to turn your template over to give you two mirror images of the dog. Cut the shapes out carefully using embroidery scissors.

2. ASSEMBLE THE DOGS

Take one felt dog piece and sew fuchsia beads on to the dog's neck to make the collar. Just below the collar in the centre, sew on a small crystal bicone bead. Finally sew on a black bead for the eye. Using a beading needle, sew the front of the dog to the back using small stitches and threading on a fuchsia bead with every stitch. Keep your beads fairly close together and make your stitches as small as possible.

Use the same technique to make up the second dog.

3. ATTACH THE DOGS TO THE GLOVES

To stop you from sewing the top and bottom of your gloves together, slide a scrunched-up plastic bag inside the glove. Thread 30cm (12in) fuchsia thread on to a beading needle and tie a knot in the end of the thread. Pin one dog on the back of a glove, go up through the glove from the inside coming out at the head of the dog, bring the needle out and go back to the right, picking up a stitch in the glove and sliding your needle through a bead. Come out two beads further on and start again. Work in this way until you have sewn on half of the dog. Tie a triple knot on the reverse and start sewing again from the top of the head, working to the left this time to attach the other side. Attach the second dog using the same technique.

4. FINISHING TOUCHES

Sew the first bone into the centre of the cuff of the glove approximately 1cm (⅜in) from the edge. Sew three crystal bicone beads each side of the bone. Sew on another bone either side of the first bone and finish by sewing a bead on each side. Make up the second glove in the same way.

Flowery fairy lights

MATERIALS REQUIRED

- Purple fairy lights
- 20 x 11cm (8in x 4¼in) synthetic felt in fuchsia
- 20 x 11cm (8in x 4¼in) synthetic felt in bright red
- 20 x 11cm (8in x 4¼in) synthetic felt in bright pink
- 20 x 11cm (8in x 4¼in) synthetic felt in mottled pink
- Mother-of-pearl beads in pale pink and dark purple
- Reel of purple brass wire
- Tube of all-purpose gel glue
- Hole punch for 20mm (¾in), 18mm (¹¹⁄₁₆in) and 2mm (³⁄₃₂in) holes
- Hammer
- Cutting mat
- Wire cutters
- Embroidery scissors

1. CUT OUT THE PIECES

The punch should give you perfect circles provided that it is used correctly. Lay the cutting mat on a flat, hard surface that is shock-resistant. A small sheet of MDF board underneath will give extra protection. To prevent wastage, draw a vertical line every 2.5cm (1in) on the surface of each of the felt pieces. Using the 20mm (¾in) punch and a hammer, make up all the rounds in this size in each of the four colours. (Remember to leave some of each colour felt for the smaller circles.) Punch the fabric within the columns you have drawn on the felt working from top to bottom. If the felt circle does not come away intact, cut it out along the markings left by the punch using embroidery scissors. Work in the same way to make up the flower centres, this time using the 18mm (¹¹⁄₁₆in) punch.

2. PUT THE FLOWERS TOGETHER

When you have cut out all the shapes, take two petals in one colour and two in another colour. Make a flower by gluing the first petal on to the second, the second on to the third, the third on to the fourth and the fourth on to the first. Alternate the colours as you go.

Finish by gluing a small circle in the third colour into the centre of the flower.

3. ASSEMBLY

When you have finished making up the flowers and the glue is dry, take the 2mm (³⁄₃₂in) punch and make a small hole in the centre of each flower. Thread a 20cm (8in) length of brass wire into a bead, and bend it back to twist it underneath the bead. Apply a little glue to the centre of a felt flower and then insert the wire into the hole in the flower so the bead sits at the centre. When the glue has dried, wind the brass wire stems of the flowers around the wire on the fairy lights.

SAHARAN TREASURES

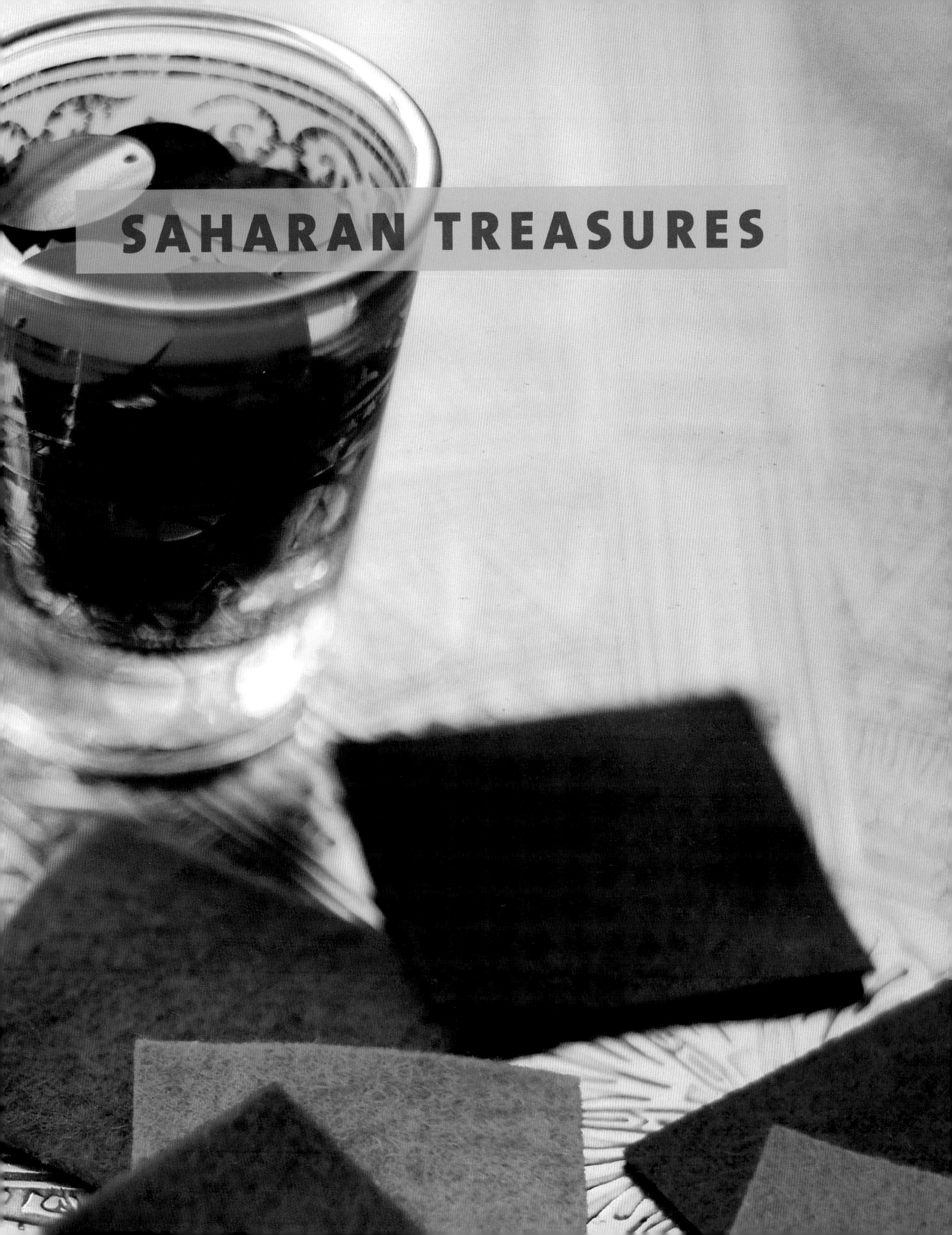

Moroccan pouffe

MATERIALS REQUIRED

- Pouffe 60cm (23½in) in diameter
- 2 x 50cm (20in) squares woven felt in red
- 50cm (20in) square lightweight iron-on fabric
- Tiny seed beads in gold
- 110cm (43⅛in) gold cord
- 75cm (29½in) gold lace braid
- Sewing thread to match the pouffe
- Sewing thread to match the red felt
- Sewing needle and beading needle
- Large-headed pins
- Fabric glue
- Soft (2B) pencil
- 50cm (20in) square sheet of tracing paper
- Bristol board
- Fine-tipped black felt-tip pen
- White gel pen
- Flat metal ruler at least 60cm (23½in) in length
- Rotary cutter
- Cutting mat
- Paper scissors and embroidery scissors
- Iron

1. MAKE UP THE MOTIF

Enlarge the central motif of the pouffe on page 97 by 220%. Trace it using a soft pencil. Iron the square of iron-on fabric on to the reverse of one of the two squares of red felt. Use a hot iron. Pin the sheet of tracing paper on to the iron-on fabric at the corners. Transfer the motif by going around the outline with a soft pencil. Remove the tracing paper. If not all of the outline is clear, turn the tracing paper over and repeat. Remove the tracing paper and go around the motif again with a black felt tip. It is crucial that the outline of the motif is clear to give you the best cutting line. Cut out the motif carefully using embroidery scissors.

2. GLUE ON THE MOTIF

Pin the motif in the dead centre of the pouffe. Stick the pins in vertically and only halfway to hold in place. Choose a place to start. Lift up a little of the felt and apply glue to the reverse, then stick it down applying a little pressure. Continue to stick down the felt a little at a time, removing the pins as you do so and leaving the pins in place on the parts that you have not yet stuck down.

Lay the tassel out on a table and choose eight of the most visible fringes. Sew small gold beads all the way down four of the strips (every other strip) using a beading needle and red thread – about 17 beads per strip.

4. MAKE UP THE SMALL MOTIFS

Trace the small motif and transfer it on to Bristol board. Cut it out. Copy the outline twelve times on the reverse of the red felt and cut the motifs out using embroidery scissors. Place the cut-out motifs around the central motif glued to the pouffe with the flat edge along the piping as if you were sticking numbers on to a clock face. Use a ruler to find the exact centre of the pouffe and place a pin in the centre. Place your first piece at 12 o'clock and the second at 6 o'clock. Hold your shapes in place with vertical pins pushed halfway in. Next, use the ruler to position the third shape at 9 o'clock and the fourth at 3 o'clock. Continue to work in this way for the remaining motifs.

To attach the shapes, lift them up without removing the pins and apply a little glue to one area on the back. Wait for two minutes, pull out the pin and apply glue to the rest of the motif.

When you have finished gluing on the motifs sew on a tassel to hang down the side between each motif. Use a small stitch to attach the tassel's gold cord to the piping around your pouffe in a thread the same colour as the pouffe.

3. MAKE THE TASSELS

To make the tassels, cut 12 rectangles measuring 12 x 12.5cm (4¾ x 4⅞in) from your second square of red felt. Using a black felt tip, draw a horizontal line on the reverse of each piece of felt 2cm (¾in) from the top. Place a rectangle right side down on a cutting mat and cut fringes every 2mm (⅛in) using a rotary cutter and a metal ruler, taking care not to cut above the black line. Always cut from the bottom to the top. You could cut the fringes with a pair of scissors, but they will not be as even. Place a rectangle with fringes right side down and apply glue to the 2cm (¾in) strip at the top which has not been cut. Cut a 9cm (3½in) length of gold cord, fold it in half to form a loop and lay the ends on the glue 1cm (⅜in) from the right edge. Add a little glue and roll the tassel up. Hold for five minutes for the glue to set. Cut a 6cm (2⅜in) length of gold lace braid. Wrap it around the top of the tassel and secure at the back with a few stitches using red thread.

Tea glass holders

MATERIALS REQUIRED

(for a tea glass 5.5cm (2¼in) in diameter)

- 28 x 8cm (11 x 3⅛in) woven felt in turquoise
- 2 pieces 17 x 8cm (6¾ x 3⅛in) synthetic felt in blue
- Seed beads in matte gold and pearlized turquoise
- Turquoise sewing thread
- Sewing needle and beading needle
- Pins
- Metallic effect stranded cotton in turquoise
- Gold fabric paint
- Very fine-tipped paintbrush
- White glue
- Spray mount adhesive
- Soft (2B) pencil
- Tracing paper
- Fine-tipped white gel pen
- Paper scissors and embroidery scissors

1. MAKE UP THE MOTIF

Enlarge the templates by 130%, then copy the shapes on to tracing paper. Cut the shapes out. Apply a little spray mount adhesive to the reverse of the stepped motifs and glue them on to the blue felt. Draw round the motifs carefully using a fine-tipped gel pen so that the outline will be precise and not too thick. Remove the template. Cut out the motif using embroidery scissors.

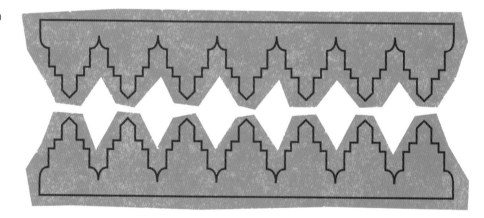

2. MAKE UP THE HOLDER

Transfer the tea glass template on to the reverse of the turquoise felt and cut it out. When you get to the handle, fold your strip of felt to cut the two handles together: this will make them identical. Lay the strip out flat, right side up, and place the top part of the stepped motif centred

along the edge of the felt. Mark where it will start and finish with two pins. Apply white glue to the reverse of the motif and stick it back down on the felt strip, using the pins as a guide. Use the same technique to attach the bottom part of the motif so that the points match. Leave the glued felt to dry for about an hour.

running stitch in
metallic effect turquoise
stranded cotton

gold fabric paint

matte gold bead

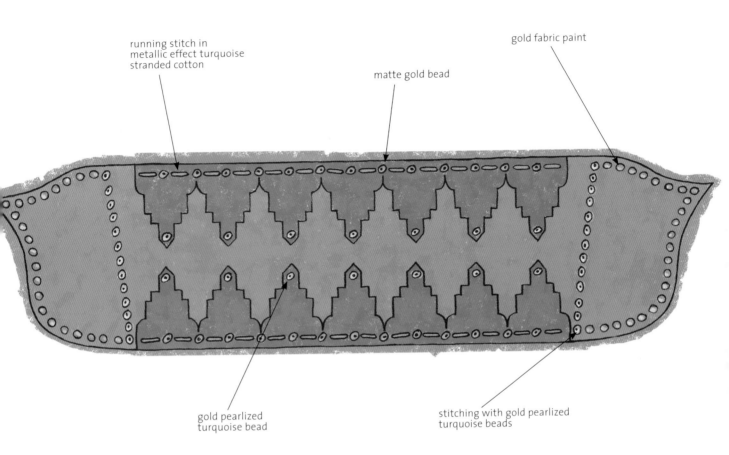

gold pearlized
turquoise bead

stitching with gold pearlized
turquoise beads

3. DECORATE THE EDGES

When the glue is dry, use metallic stranded cotton and
a fairly long running stitch to join the two layers of felt
together (see page 13). Stitch close to the edge along the
top and bottom edges of the motif adding a matte gold
bead between each running stitch along both edges. Sew
turquoise beads on to the points of the top and bottom
motifs using turquoise thread.

4. ASSEMBLY

Wrap the holder around the tea glass. Mark where the
stitching will go with a pin. The holder should fit very
snugly around the glass. Secure with a running stitch in
turquoise thread, and then sew turquoise beads along the
stitching line on each side. Using a fine-tipped paintbrush,
dot gold fabric glue around the outside edge of each
handle. Leave to dry for at least one hour.

North African cake tray

MATERIALS REQUIRED

- 50cm (20in) square woven felt in turquoise
- 50cm (20in) square woven felt in brown
- 4 x 26cm (1½ x 10⅛in) woven felt in brown
- 2 x 50cm (20in) squares and a strip 3 x 12cm (1⅛ x 4¾in) medium-weight double-sided iron-on fabric
- Seed beads in brown and transparent gold
- Sewing thread in turquoise and brown
- Sewing needle and beading needle
- Pins
- Spray mount adhesive
- Soft (2B) pencil
- Tracing paper
- 50cm (20in) sheet Bristol board
- Ball-point pen
- Fabric pen
- Paper scissors and embroidery scissors
- Iron

1. MAKE UP THE BASKET MOTIF

Enlarge the template on page 105 by 215%, trace and cut it out. Apply a little spray mount adhesive to the back of the template and glue it on to Bristol board to secure it while you transfer the motif. If you do not have a large sheet of Bristol board, join sheets with sticky tape. Copy the outline of the template using a ball-point pen and cut it out. Place the Bristol board template on the reverse of the brown felt and draw around the outline using a fabric pen. Repeat this process on the turquoise felt. Cut the two shapes out carefully using embroidery scissors.

2. PUT THE MOTIF TOGETHER

Cut two 24cm (9½in) squares from the iron-on fabric and 20 small rectangles measuring 3cm x 5mm (1⅛ x ³⁄₁₆in). You will use these small supports to strengthen the sides of your tray. Lay the brown felt motif right side down and place the two squares of iron-on fabric in the centre. Next, place small supports down the centre of all the side motifs, using the diagram as a guide. Place the turquoise felt motif right side up with the reverse against the iron-on fabric on the brown felt.

Make sure the iron-on fabric is correctly centred – there should be no fabric sticking out at the sides. Use a very hot iron with the steam setting turned off to set your work. The iron-on fabric will take effect only once your felt has completely cooled down.

3. DECORATE THE TRAY

Using brown thread and a beading needle, sew a running stitch around the outside of the motif to secure the two pieces of felt together (see page 13). With each stitch, thread on a brown seed bead on the outside and space the stitches/beads at about 5mm (³⁄₁₆in) intervals. Try to sew between the felt layers to avoid stitches showing on the inside of the tray.

4. MAKE UP THE SMALL MOTIFS

Trace the template of the small motif and transfer it on to a piece of Bristol board. Cut out the shape and copy it twelve times on the reverse of the brown felt using a fabric pen. Cut out the motifs using embroidery scissors. Pin them in the places indicated by a star on the diagram. Sew them on using a small stitch and a beading needle, adding gold seed beads at the points. Try to sew between the two pieces of felt so that the stitches do not show on the inside of the tray.

5. MAKE UP THE TRAY

Use turquoise thread to sew the four corners of the basket together with a double row of stitches, the first at the edge and the second about 1cm (³⁄₈in) from the edge. Next, sew a tight close running stitch around the base of the tray to create a pronounced edge. This will add body to the tray. Finish by attaching the corner motifs at the sides and tips as shown in the diagram.

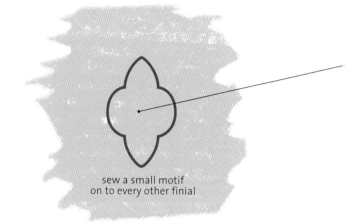

sew a small motif
on to every other finial

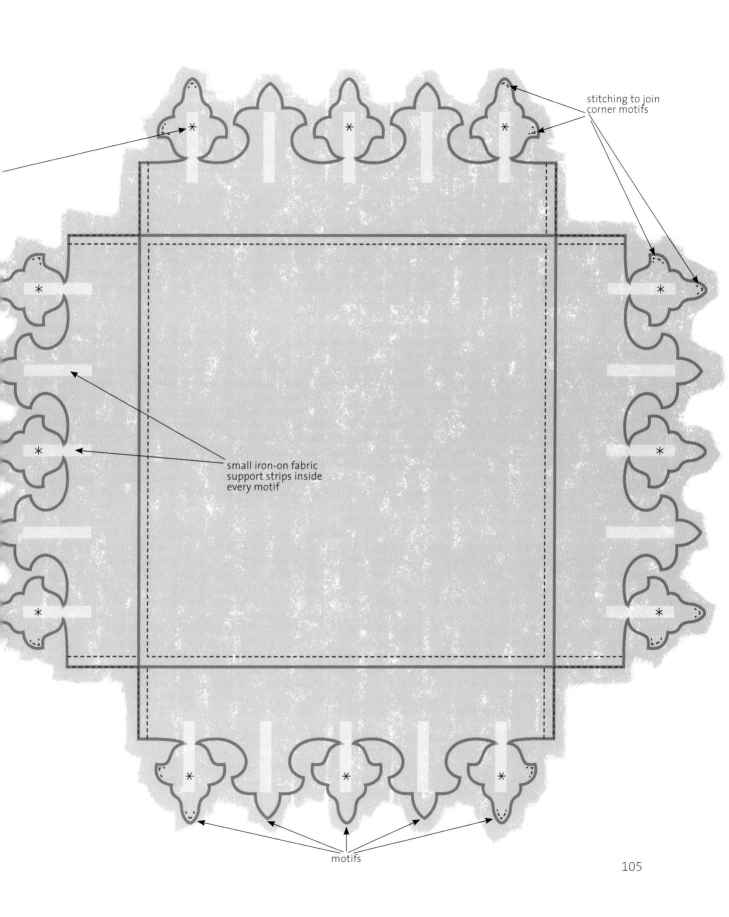

stitching to join
corner motifs

small iron-on fabric
support strips inside
every motif

motifs

105

Jewelled candleholders

MATERIALS REQUIRED

- 28 x 30cm (11 x 12in) sheet clear adhesive-backed plastic
- 3 pieces 28 x 11cm (11 x 4¼in) polyester netting in gold
- Sewing threads to match the felt
- Sewing needle
- All-purpose gel glue
- Spray mount adhesive
- White glue
- Fine-tipped paintbrush
- Soft (2B) pencil
- Tracing paper
- Thin Bristol board
- White gel pen
- Cutting mat
- Flat metal ruler
- Rotary cutter
- Pinking shears
- Paper scissors and embroidery scissors
- Iron

CANDLEHOLDER A

- 28 x 10cm (11 x 4in) synthetic felt in copper
- 6 x 7cm (2⅜ x 2¾in) synthetic felt in fuchsia
- 4 drop beads in amber
- 3 faceted beads in red and gold
- 4 gold sequins
- 60cm (23½in) sequin tape in brown
- 30cm (12in) sequin tape in fuchsia

CANDLEHOLDER B

- 28 x 10cm (11 x 4in) synthetic felt in fuchsia
- 6 x 7cm (2⅜ x 2¾in) synthetic felt in copper
- 4 gold sequins
- 6 faceted beads in red and gold
- 60cm (23½in) sequin tape in brown

CANDLEHOLDER C

- 28 x 10cm (11 x 4in) synthetic felt in chilli red
- 6 x 7cm (2⅜ x 2¾in) synthetic felt in fuchsia
- 4 gold sequins
- 65cm (25½in) sequinned braid 9mm (²³⁄₆₄in) wide in brown

1. PREPARE THE CANDLEHOLDERS

Lay the sheet of plastic on a cutting mat and cut three rectangles measuring 28 x 10cm (11 x 4in) using a rotary cutter and a metal ruler for a neat finish.

If you do not have a cutter and mat, cut the rectangles out carefully using sharp scissors, trying to avoid making unnecessary nicks in the plastic. Iron the three pieces of gold netting with a warm iron. Using pinking shears, trim each piece to give you three rectangles 26 x 11cm (10⅛ x 4¼in). Remove the backing from 26cm (10⅛in) of your plastic and stick on the gold netting, smoothing out any creases as you go. Use pinking shears to trim any excess fabric from the top and the bottom.

Candleholder B

Candleholder A

2. ATTACH THE BRAID OR SEQUIN TAPE

Depending on which candleholder you are making, take the sequin tape or braid. Cut 30cm (12in) lengths and remove the sequins from each end to expose 2cm (¾in) of thread. Tie a small knot at each end and trim the threads close to the knot. Using the diagrams as a guide, work out where the braid or tape will go and apply a little gel glue. Stick on the tape or braid carefully so as not to get glue on the sequins. Should this happen, allow the glue to dry and scrape it off carefully with a knife.

3. MAKE UP THE MOTIFS

Enlarge the motifs by 140%. Trace them and transfer them on to the Bristol board. Cut them out using paper scissors, removing the middle sections carefully. Place each motif on the reverse of the respective felt rectangle. Draw round the outlines of the different motifs using a gel pen.

Cut the three large felt motifs out using embroidery scissors. Then, using the colours on the diagram as a guide, cut out the small felt motifs.

4. DECORATE THE MOTIFS

Sew beads or sequins on to the different pieces of felt. For candleholder C, take the sequins off the remaining length of braid and put them aside. Apply a little spray mount to the reverse of the felt motifs and position them on the gold net-covered plastic. When you are happy with the overall effect, lift up your motifs a little at a time and apply a little white glue using a paintbrush. Leave to dry for at least an hour and use gel glue to attach sequins to the felt on candleholder B and candleholder C.

5. FINISHING TOUCHES

Remove the 2cm (¾in) of backing that you left on the plastic. Put the candleholder together, overlapping the two ends and pressing down firmly. Add a little gel glue if necessary. Put a tealight in a glass yoghurt pot and place in the centre of the candleholder.

Candleholder C

A

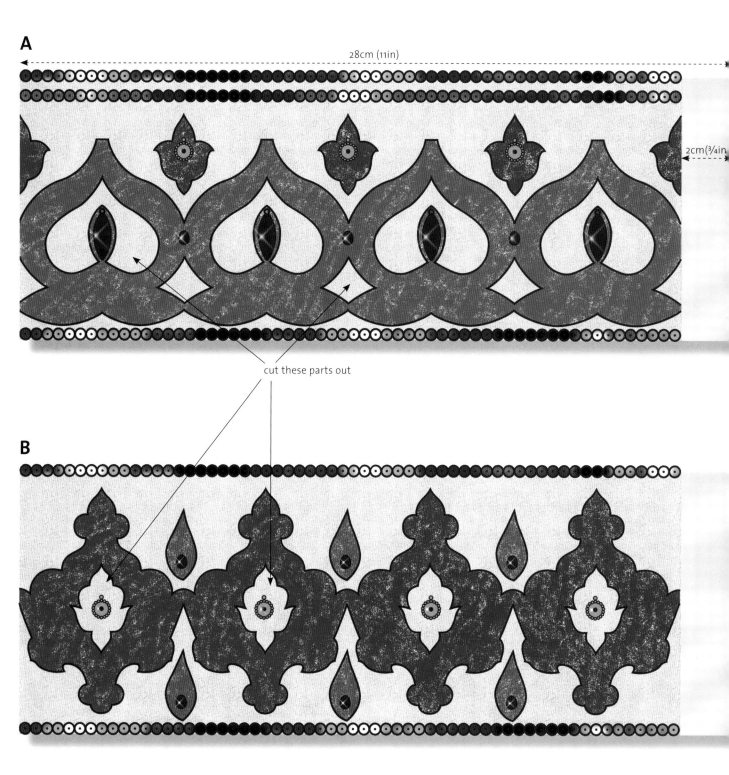

28cm (11in)

2cm (¾in)

cut these parts out

B

cut these parts out

 sequinned braid in brown

 sequin tape in brown

 sequin tape in fuchsia

 motifs in fuchsia felt

 motifs in copper felt

 motifs in chilli red felt

 sequins taken from braid to be glued on to the felt

 amber beads

 faceted beads in red and gold

 gold sequins

111

Hand of Fatima talisman

MATERIALS REQUIRED

- 26cm (10⅛in) square woven felt in henna
- 22 x 14cm (8⅝ x 5½in) woven felt in mahogany
- 4 silver costume beads
- Seed beads in matte silver
- 6 large beads in matte red
- 20cm (8in) silver lurex cord
- 1 x 12cm (4¾in) tassel
- Sewing thread to match your felt
- Silver stranded cotton
- Sewing needle, chenille needle, beading needle
- Tube silver relief paint
- Fabric glue
- Punch
- Pencil
- Tracing paper
- White gel pen
- Paper scissors and embroidery scissors

1. CUT OUT THE MOTIFS

Enlarge the three motifs by 145% and copy them on to
tracing paper separately. Cut them out. Lay the large
motif and the hand on the reverse of the henna felt and
the small motif on the reverse of the mahogany felt. Draw
round the outlines using a gel pen. Cut the motifs out
inside the markings using embroidery scissors.

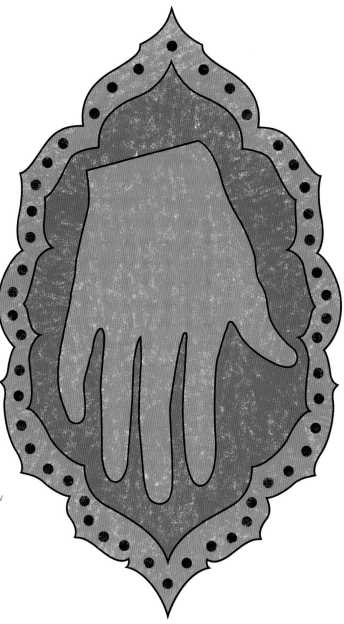

112

2. MAKE UP THE BRACELETS

Use the picture as a guide to making up the two bracelets.
Thread a needle with henna thread and tie a knot in the
end. Thread the needle through from the back of the fabric,
3mm (⅛in) from the edge of the wrist on the left-hand
side, to the right side of the fabric and thread on the red
beads and costume beads as indicated. Go back through
the fabric on the right of the wrist, come out at the
back and tie a knot to secure the bracelet. Use the same
technique to make up the shorter seed bead bracelet, this
time using a beading needle, and to make the ring.

3. DECORATE THE MOTIFS

Run a couching stitch around the edge of the mahogany
felt shape using six strands of silver stranded cotton
for the laid thread and one strand, threaded through a
chenille needle, for the tying stitch (see page 13). Place
the hand of Fatima in the centre of this piece of felt and
sew the two layers together with a running stitch around
the edge of the hand (see page 13). Go around the outline
of the large henna felt shape using silver relief paint and
leave to dry for two hours. Make holes all around the motif
using a punch. Do not make the holes too regular; try to
capture something of the spirit of a hand-crafted piece.

4. ASSEMBLY

Apply glue to the reverse of the mahogany felt with the
hand sewn on and place it on the large motif. Loop lurex
cord around the tassel and attach it to the back.

Moroccan slippers

MATERIALS REQUIRED

- Pair fuchsia slippers
- 25 x 18cm (9⅞ x 7in) woven felt in purple
- 17 x 24cm (6¾ x 9½in) synthetic felt in violet
- Violet glitter paint
- Fine-tipped paintbrush
- Water-based gouache varnish (optional)
- Fabric glue
- Soft (2B) pencil
- Tracing paper
- 2 x A4 sheets Bristol board
- White gel pen
- Flat metal ruler
- Rotary cutter
- Cutting mat
- Paper scissors and embroidery scissors

1. CUT OUT THE MOTIFS

Enlarge the three templates by 110% and copy them on to tracing paper. Use a ruler to draw the straight edges of the bead. Transfer the motifs on to Bristol board and cut them out. Place templates A and B on the reverse of the purple felt and draw round the outlines twice using a white gel pen. Place the bead template on the violet felt and make six copies. Cut out motifs A and B using embroidery scissors. Use a rotary cutter, ruler and cutting mat to cut a neater line for the bead motifs.

2. PAINT THE MOTIFS

Using a fine-tipped paintbrush, apply a thin line of glitter paint around the outside edge of each piece, on the right side of the fabric. Try not to make the line too thick; instead make it thin and go over it again if necessary. Leave to dry for at least two hours and then apply a thin layer of water-based gouache varnish over the glitter paint to set it.

3. MAKE THE BEADS

Apply a stripe of glue to the back of each bead motif and roll the felt up, starting from the widest end. Hold the bead for a few minutes while the glue takes hold.

4. ATTACH THE MOTIFS

Apply glue to the reverse of motifs A and B, then stick the pieces on to the slippers in the following order: top bead, motif B at the tip of the slipper, motif A and then the two remaining beads.

bead

motif B

motif A

DESIGNS

INTO THE WOODS

Festive heart (page 16)

Irish table runner (page 18)

Beaded tieback (page 20)

BACK TO NATURE

Heart candleholder (page 38)

Angel Christmas stocking (page 40)

Frosted wreath (page 42)

Edelweiss flower ball (page 44)

Pansy photo mount (page 24)

Iris throw (page 26)

Cuckoo clock (page 30)

Winter warmer (page 46)

Season's Greetings (page 50)

Christmas photo album (page 52)

Silver snowflakes (page 54)

PASTEL PALETTE

Swallow cushion (page 58)

Butterfly lampshade (page 60)

Baby's first book (page 64)

Angel baby blanket (page 66)

OVER THE RAINBOW

Party bags (page 82)

Bear cub Alice bands (page 84)

Strawberry hairclips and hair band (page 86)

SAHARAN TREASURES

Moroccan pouffe (page 94)

Tea glass holders (page 98)

North African cake tray (page 102)

Toy box (page 68)

Doll's vanity case (page 74)

Floral cushion (page 76)

Puppy gloves (page 88)

Flowery fairy lights (page 90)

Jewelled candleholders (page 106)   Hand of Fatima talisman (page 112)   Moroccan slippers (page 114)

SUPPLIERS' ADDRESSES

Haberdashery departments and specialist craft and sewing shops sell felt, embroidery threads and dressmaking materials and equipment. There are also specialist suppliers:

United Kingdom

ArtyMiss,
51 Huggets Lane,
Eastbourne,
East Sussex BN22 0LT
01323 504896
www.artymiss.co.uk

Craft Bits
1 Barncroft Villas,
Manor House Street
Peterborough, PE1 2TL
01733 566617
www.craftbits.co.uk

Fun2Do,
2 Scotch Street,
Carlisle, CA3 8PY
01228 528343
www.fun2do.co.uk

Hardy & Hanson,
Longlands Road,
Staincliffe,
Dewsbury,
West Yorkshire WF13 4AB
01924 462353
www.hardy-hanson.co.uk

Hobbycraft
Stores throughout UK
www.hobbycraft.co.uk

Time to Change Fabrics
33 Church Street,
Alloa, FK10 1DH
01259 218844
www.time2changefabrics.co.uk

Torbay Textiles
7 Hilton Drive
Preston, Paignton,
Devon, TQ31 1JW
01803 522673
www.torbaytextiles.co.uk

USA

A Child's Dream Come True
1223 D Michigan Street
Sandpoint, ID 83864
800-359-2906
www.achildsdream.com

Aetna Felt Corp.
2401 W. Emaus Avenue,
Allentown, PA 18103
1--800-526-4451
www.aetnafelt.com

CPE Felt
541 Buffalo West Springs Highway,
Union, SC 29379
800-327-0059
www.cpe-felt.com

Felt Pro
479-790-5079
www.feltpro.net/default.html

Jo-Ann Stores
Craft shops nationwide
www.joann.com

Mister Art
913 Willard Street,
Houston, TX 77006
800-721-3015
www.misterart.com

Vogue Fabrics,
718-732 Main Street,
Evanston, IL-60202
1-800-433-4313
www.voguefabricstore.com